Collana
ART IN N. 2

Cover:
Jaen Anderson

Printed in Italy by
C.M.T., Milan
August 1988

N
7277
B37
1988

A M N O N   B A R Z E L

A *i* R *n* T
ISRAEL

Flash Art
BOOKS

GIANCARLO POLITI EDITORE

Chapter I

The Founding Generation: 1906-1919

The beginnings and development of art in Eretz-Israel (Palestine) are unique in their capacity to indicate an exact date for the rise of art in an emerging nation.

The year 1906 marks the starting point. This was the year that the Bezalel Academy of Art was founded; a singular institution of secular higher education, in a city with a Jewish population of 35,000 souls out of a total of 60,000 inhabitants, in a far-flung province of the Ottoman Empire. The founding of Bezalel was part of the Zionist settlement process in Eretz-Israel, and the decision for its establishment was made in the framework of the Fifth Zionist Congress, convened in Basel in 1901.

The existence of a nucleus of Western art in Ottoman Palestine makes it possible to follow the development of Israeli art as one would follow a laboratory process, parallel to the Zionist settlement of Jews in Palestine implanting Western culture in the East.

The style created in Bezalel from 1906 to 1920 and afterwards reflects the problems and ideals which accompanied the Jewish national movement. This movement was dedicated to the return of the Jewish people to their home and to the creation of "a new individual and a new society in a new land"; it sought the solution to the problems of the Jews as an exiled people subject to the persecution of anti-semitism. The work and vision of Herzl, "seer of the Jewish State," came into being with the immigration to and settlement of Eretz-Israel mostly by Jews of Eastern and Central Europe. The founding of the Bezalel Academy provided an educational and spiritual nucleus in the settlement of Israel. Accordingly, the growth of

art in Eretz-Israel derived from the needs, contents, and ideals of Zionist Jewry in Europe. It saw its task as that of cultivating the Jewish community in Palestine and of building up a new Jewish-European culture that would be sensitive to Eastern influences yet dependent on a new reality arising from the history of the people forged and formulated in what was Eretz-Israel. Creative art in Eretz-Israel fought for the realization of this definition from the very outset, in the first decade of the Twentieth Century. The formation of a nucleus of art in Eretz-Israel—in the form of the Bezalel School for Arts and Crafts in Jerusalem—was, as we have mentioned, part a major political undertaking, a national Jewish endeavour; and whatever was achieved in this artistic framework came to serve the Zionist enterprise, without being an organic requisite of Ottoman Jerusalem in the first decades of the Twentieth Century.

The establishment of the Bezalel School centre was primarily the project of one man: Boris Schatz, a Jewish artist of deep Zionistic proclivities. Born in Lithuania in 1866, Schatz first studied in his native land and in Warsaw, reaching Paris in 1889 to study with the sculptor Antokolsky. Under his influence, and in the pathetic heroic spirit of nationalism prevalent at the end of the Nineteenth Century (particularly in Jewish artistic circles in Europe), Schatz created a historical sculpture symbolizing the prophets of the Bible and the freedom fighters in Jewish history before the people were exiled from their homeland.

In 1896 Boris Schatz joined the founders of the Royal Academy of Art in the capital of Bulgaria, established at the initiative of Duke Ferdinand. The six years he spent in Bulgaria—cooperating in the founding of the Academy and in the encouragement of the undertaking to bring popular art to the villages—was of decisive importance to his move to establish an arts-and-crafts centre in Jerusalem, as well as to the objectives of this artistic-national nucleus.

The Jewish national awakening at the end of the Nineteenth Century, which was dedicated to the restoration of the people to its historical homeland in Eretz-Israel, also regarded the improvement of the individual and the creation of a new type of Jew as one of the basic conditions for the realization of the Zionist Vision. This conception gave high priority to the evolution of a new culture in Eretz-Israel. At the Zionist Congress in Basel, in 1901, Schatz put forth the resolution approving the founding of Bezalel as the first and only institute of secular higher learning in Palestine. The Hebrew University and the Haifa Technion were founded only some twenty years later.

The establishment of the Bezalel school therefore conformed with the Zionist objectives of making Eretz-Israel the spiritual centre of the people, encouraging settlement, and providing sources of livelihood in the "have-not" country. In the utopian and idealistic vision of the return to Eretz-Israel, the concept of human self-improvement and the emergence of a new Jew on his soil greatly engaged the thinking of Jewish intellectuals and Zionist leadership—Theodor Herzl, Max Nordau, Ahad Ha'am, and many others—in the early years of the century. Martin Buber, appearing at the Zionist Congress in 1901, called for the establishment of a creative-art centre in Eretz-Israel: "National art must have the soil from which it will grow, and the skies toward which it will send its blossoms. We, the Jews of today, have neither of these. National art must have a homogeneous human society, from which it originates and for which it exists. Perfect Jewish art can transpire only on Jewish soil, as must all Jewish culture in general." An exhibit of famed Jewish artists of that period—Lesser Uri, Herman Struck, Yosef Israels, Moritz Gottlieb, Ephraim Lilien, and others—was mounted in the building in which the congress was held, reflecting the consent of Zionism's leaders to the establishment of an arts-and-crafts centre in the new land.

E.M. LILIEN, POSTCARD EDITED FOR THE 5TH ZIONIST CONGRESS IN BASEL, DECEMBER 1901.
COURTESY Z. ALEXANDER.

6

"בְּצַלְאֵל"

בֵּית מִדְרָשׁ לִמְלָאכוֹת אָמָנוּת

BEZALEL
Kunstgewerbeschule
Jerusalem.

BEZALEL SYMBOL ON STATIONARY, JERUSALEM, c. 1910.

In 1904, Boris Schatz submitted his plan to Herzl and received approval for the founding of Bezalel. Schatz arrived in Jerusalem a year later and immediately proceeded to the practical stage, with the Bulgarian Academy serving him as a model.

There remained the question of what function the Bezalel Academy was to fill within the historical framework of the political utopia of the Jewish people. The complexity of the answer requires an assessment of the Zionist-Jewish utopia situation, on one hand, and the state of matters in Jerusalem, in 1906, on the other. Bezalel was designed to be one of the instruments in the shaping of a new Jew in a new land, counter-balancing the Diaspora; as one of Herzl's aides put it, "a new generation of Jews, different from all previous generations, with new courage in its spirit and new thinking in its brain"; to form a synthesis of the European spirit and the Jewish: "Proud and courageous is the Jew, moral and social as he reverts to himself and recognizes his ego." Bezalel was to change the gamut of occupations for the new Jew. The creative skills and professions, the development of craftsmanship and a sense of aesthetics—these are often mentioned in the writings of contemporary Zionist philosophers.

Jerusalem was at that time a small Jewish community, economically atrophied, living mostly within the walls of the old city. It was a pious community, existing in a meagre fashion on the donations sent from religious centres in the Diaspora. A province of the Turkish Empire, it was ruled by fear. Its 35,000 Jews and 25,000 Moslems hardly knew of any secular culture. The same was true of the 15,000 Jews living in Jaffa, Hebron, Tiberias, Safed, and the sprinkling in the farming communities, the first of which was founded in 1878.

Given this background in Jerusalem, and the complete financial dependence of Bezalel on the Jewish establishment in Europe (the Berlin Committee headed by Professor Warburg), the school was founded as an instruction centre for crafts and handiwork— actually a complex of workshops for carpet weaving and goldsmith work, olive-wood carving, enamelling, and ivory work. The need to strengthen the Academy's economic basis led it to become a network of profitable workshops, to provide jobs for the city's inhabitants and to turn them into creative artisans. The original purpose of establishing an art centre was put aside.

Bezalel is an unusual example of the precedent for creating a new people and an outpost of Western culture in the East. The motivation remained constant—to create a new Hebrew culture, based on Jewish values and Hebrew roots in the historical homeland, roots leading to the Bible, synthesizing with the culture of the East. This was the spiritual

7

and philosophical ideal behind the establishment of Bezalel. But what happened to this purpose and its intimation of a Jewish renaissance?

Boris Schatz as an artist was an uncompromising academician, totally antagonistic towards new currents. To him, the creation of a new art in Eretz-Israel had to develop along academic lines, rather than proposing a new style that would synthesize nationalistic content with Eastern influences. The Bezalel style was eclectic, the result of extreme idealism, utopian-zionism, attached to Jewish culture abroad but aspiring to be local and Eastern. Actually, Bezalel created and fostered national and local symbols, such as the *menorah* (candelabrum). (This ritual item originating in the Biblical account of the formation of Jewry in the desert, following the exodus from Egypt, was later to become the emblem of the State of Israel). Among similar manifestations were the stylized Star of David, the use of the palm tree, Eastern headgear, the Western Wall, the camel, and, above all, the idealization of Eretz-Israel as an ancient biblical paradise. The Jugendstil,

inspired by Lilien and later by Zeev Raban, depicted ideals of Judaism liberated and Herzl as a prophet or as a sun. There were illustrations of biblical passages ("for from Zion shall come forth learning"). The present and its demands turned into an ancient Jugenstiel biblical reality, and Hebrew letters interwoven with drawings and designs were also made into an imaginative art nouveau. Everything became an intermingling in festivity—Persian rugs and miniatures alongside European baroque and Islamic arabesque, echoes of illuminated Jewish manuscripts, and the tradition of Jewish-Yemenite ornamentation alongside Western filigree.

The founders of Bezalel obviously had a problem—they dreamed and longed for Zion, while they actually lived in Jerusalem. The land where the episodes described in the *Song of Songs* transpired and where the tribes of Israel settled was now before their eyes. It was not the wonderful biblical landscape their books predicted, but a scorched land. Their only escape lay in idealizing reality. The pious Jews of Jerusalem, Ashkenazi and Sephardi, the "old-timers," did not seem

BORIS SCHATZ, THE MARRIAGE-BROKER,
BEZALEL EPOCH.

BORIS SCHATZ, THE PROPHET ISAIAH,
BEZALEL EPOCH.

much different from the diasporic dwellers of the ghettoes whom they had left behind in order to generate the new Jew. Hence they regarded the Arabs and the Bedouins living in Palestine as representatives of the biblical images, as the Jews of the past in Eretz-Israel.

This eclecticism became the style characteristic of the initial stage of Hebrew creative art in Eretz-Israel. It may not have provided an accurate depiction of the land, but it did express an escape to a dream fashioned out of fragments of hope and naïve enthusiasm, to the "beclouded rosy utopia" of Boris Schatz and his colleagues, and to Herzl's romantic utopia, as he described it in his *Altneuland* in 1902.

However, in an idealistic society which sees in its activities a change in the historical progress of Judaism, there can be no talk of an esoteric art enclosed within the problem of art *per se*. Bezalel was supposed to create a national style, in addition to being an economic instrument. In other words, it was to be a pioneering enterprise, an extention of the Zionist movement in Europe, absolutely dependent upon the institutions of the movement. The dependence was idealistic as well as economic. In the writings of contemporary leaders, men of letters and journalists, including the school's *Declaration of Intentions*, we find the unequivocal idea that "Bezalel is the solution to the desperate situation of jobs and livelihoods in Eretz-Israel," not only for city dwellers, but also for farmers, whom the crafts would help in times of drought or crop failure.

In his enthusiasm, Schatz also clung to the idea, popular in Europe in the second half of the Nineteenth Century, that handicrafts would rescue the human being from the pressure of mechanization and the erosion of the worker's personality. John Ruskin's philosophy, which called for an imperative change in man's life styles if he was to be aroused to a sensitivity toward beauty and art, struck a responsive chord in Schatz's practical ideology, and contributed in no small measure to the founding of Bezalel as a professional manual-labour-training centre for the Jewish community in Jerusalem, as a precondition for the stage of creating a spiritual and artistic centre. In the depressed economic state of Ottoman Jerusalem in 1906,

E.M. LILIEN, MOSES ON MOUNT SINAI, 1908.
(HERZEL AS MODEL FOR THE PORTRAIT OF MOSES).

the establishment of workshops for handicrafts—weaving, carving, smithing, and the like—was a brilliant idea, economically as well as from the viewpoint of the creation of national stylistic motifs. What is more, the idea of establishing a crafts school while toning down and shunting the fine-arts facet appealed to the Zionist Congress in Europe, particularly to the Berlin Zionist Committee, with which Schatz was in direct contact for the funding of the Academy (following the death of Herzl, the president of the Zionist Congresses, in 1904). Indeed, the resolution to establish the school was a political decision, and Bezalel had to justify its existence as an instrument for the settlement of Jews in Zion, primarily as an economic factor, while serving as an important institution of cultural improvement. Schatz's statements concerning the remendous importance of the cottage crafts, vis-à-vis the mechanization which was destroying the worker's spiritual base and alienating him from the work of his hands, were intended to hit both targets: an economic solution and human improvement in Eretz-Israel. Thus Schatz was carried along on the romantic clouds which characterized Ruskin's philosophy, which envisioned redemption from technology in manual work and cottage crafts, in the existence of the guilds, and in the revival of production as it was in the Middle Ages. The dependence of Bezalel on the Jewish bourgeoisie in Europe made it difficult to identify Schatz with the radical socialist William Morris, or with the Arts and Crafts circles which he prompted. Nevertheless, documents relevant to the first years of Bezalel hint at a certain friction between Schatz and the Berlin Committee, which argued that "art may be studied anywhere, but national crafts should and must be done in Jerusalem."

We are talking here about the development of Bezalel as part of the process of implanting Western culture in the East—in Palestine, which, from the stand point of Western culture, was then, at the turn of the century, a desolate wilderness. The founders of Bezalel therefore had to create an "environment" at the very outset. Schatz proceeded to lay the foundation for a museum, which at first contained a collection of Jewish art and local archeological finds. He set up a library

E.M. LILIEN, THE WAILING WALL, JERUSALEM, 1910.

of art books such as were hardly to be found in Jerusalem in those days, a collection of stuffed animals, evening sessions of listening to recorded classics, and a choral ensemble. Most of all, he declared Hebrew to be the sole language of instruction at Bezalel. Indeed, one of his supporters in Jerusalem was Eliezer Ben-Yehuda, the intellectual credited with the revival of the Hebrew language in Eretz-Israel. After all, one of the aims of the Zionist movement was the normalization of the Jewish people by having it "dwell in one land and have one language of its own."

Bezalel, then, was more than a school for the arts and crafts. It was a pendulum that swung toward a new social order. In this context, Boris Schatz founded a village for Jewish artists (most of them arrivals from Yemen), silversmiths, and workers in fine metals, and he planned to establish another in the Jerusalem area. In 1909, when 150 people were already in the workshops, he arranged exhibitions in the young farming settlements. Bezalel creations were also displayed in Odessa, then an important Zionist centre, and in the foyers of the Zionist Congresses in Basel. Schatz created an all-encompassing socio-cultural environment and even established a student commune financially aided by the school. The problem Schatz had to face was to have accomplished artists who would join him in laying the basis for art in Palestine, for settlement in the "artistic desert" of Ottoman Jerusalem at the beginning of the century was contrary to the logic of the artistic ego.

Schatz arrived in Jerusalem in 1906. With him were Ephraim Lilien, a Jugenstiel artist from Vienna with a fine reputation (his influence dominated the formation of the Bezalel style), and the German-Jewish painter Rothschild, whose contribution and artistry cannot now be identified. A year later significant reinforcements arrived, in the persons of the painter Shmuel Hirschenberg, known in the Jewish world for his monumental national-religious works (he was at Bezalel for a year, until his death); and of the painter Lachovsky. Later came the painter Krestin. In 1913, the group was joined by Abel Pann and Aharon Shaul Schor.

In addition to the objective difficulties

ABEL PANN, THE SYNAGOGUE, AFTER THE POGROM. 1916. COLLECTION ISRAEL MUSEUM, JERUSALEM.

which beset Bezalel and Jerusalem, the school suffered the loss of its artist-instructors (Lilien, Krestin, Lachovsky, Abel Pann—the latter returned only in 1920). They left because Bezalel was engaging mostly in crafts, and the art academy was merely a dream in a better future. Many of the first students—Ben-David, Raban, Shmuel Levy-Ophel, Harubi, Gur-Arye—became teachers.

Other students who enrolled in Bezalel in the second decade of the century (most of them came to the country for the purpose of study, particularly from Eastern Europe) found themselves in workshops for design, fine smith work, weaving, or carving ivory. All of them left the school, and most of them returned to their lands of origin. Many, however—including Reuven Rubin, Paldi, Menahem Shemi, Litvinovsky, Agadati—came back and continued with art early in the 1920s. They formed the focus of the second chapter in the history of Eretz-Israeli art.

Theodor Herzl came to Zionism, according to his own testimony, as a result of the Dreyfus trial in 1894, as well as of the anti-semitic writings of Diring and the Frenchman Drimond (1892). He wrote: "We want to give the Jews a homeland, not by uprooting them forcibly from their native soil, but by removing them carefully, with their roots intact, in order to transplant them in better soil."

The problems inherent in transplanting this culture sharply accompanied the na-tional-cultural endeavour to create a new art in Eretz-Israel. This creativity, in the first two decades of the present century centred on Bezalel. The problems persisted in the 1920s, 1930s and 1940s, and their echoes are felt even today. The result of the searching, the arguments and contradictions, the confusion in the demarcation of Judaism as a nationality and a religion at one and the same time, the return to the East and the search for roots in ancient myths, the attempt to translate biblical images into modern verbalization and the obligation toward Jewish culture created in the Diaspora, social and Zionist idealism—all these are but part of the essence which created the Bezalel style, whose eclecticism is an original stylistic phenomenon, a rare attestation to the first twenty years of a Jewish renaissance in Palestine.

The Bezalel arts-and-crafts school was not the sole extension sponsored by the Zionist movement for the establishment of a spiritual centre in the land. In 1907, in the Neveh-Zedek quarter (the first Jewish neighborhood outside Jaffa), a literary periodical, "Haomer," made its appearance, edited by Sh. Ben-Zion. "Haomer" represented an attempt to transfer the literary centre of the Hebrew language from Eastern Europe, particularly Odessa, to Eretz-Israel; but the population was sparse and concentrated mainly in Jerusalem and in Jaffa and the few rural communities recently founded in the country. The chroniclers of literature in Eretz-Israel note the year 1907 as the beginning of Hebrew literature there, just as the founding of Bezalel marks the beginning of art in Eretz-Israel. "Haomer" was founded due to the influence of Ahad Ha'am (Asher Ginsburg), the writer and philospher, one of the outstanding intellectuals in the Zionist centre of Odessa. He was the exponent of one of the subtrends in Zionism, which sought a change in the spirit of the people which would create a spiritual centre in Eretz-Israel even before substantial steps were taken to settle on its soil.

Boris Schatz (and with him, the influential artist Ephraim Lilien during his brief stay in Eretz-Israel) was close to the editor of "Haomer," and was likewise influenced by Ahad Ha'am, (who demanded that Jewish nationalist sculptor Antokolsky make histor-

SHMUEL HIRSHENBERG, THE WAY TO THE WAILING
WALL, JERUSALEM, 1906.

ical Jewish figures and cease creating images
of bishops, for example). In Palestine itself,
criticism of the periodical was voiced on the
grounds that it expressed ideology and content germane to the Diaspora, completely
ignoring the spirit and atmosphere in the land
and its new social reality—the same criticism
that was levelled at Bezalel.

In 1907, the year which witnessed the
appearance of "Haomer", another periodical
was launched, "Hapoel Hatzair," reflecting
socialist Zionism. Indeed, in 1904 came the
"Second Aliya," recorded in Jewish history as
the launching of the Socialist Age of Pioneering. The Second Aliya was the outcome of the
wave of anti-semitism which culminated in
the Kishinev pogroms and the ensuing failure
of the 1905 revolution in Russia, causing
havoc, persecution, and the massacre of Jews.

Socialist Zionist immigration led to "a
new race of the Hebrew toiler on his soil."
Religion was replaced by the cult of labour,
and the existence of this race was predicated
on a negation of the Diaspora, as voiced by
David Ben-Gurion, one of the new arrivals:
"Our movement is the result of the rebellion
carried out by socialist youth against the sup-
pressive Jewish experience, in the miserable
reality of exile." The Second Aliya people
drained swamps, laid roads, established
kibbutzim—the farm communes (the first
was founded in 1909 on the banks of the Sea

of Galilee)—and became the extreme antithesis to traditional and bourgeois Judaism, the
paternal generation in Eastern Europe. Compared with this ideology and style of life, the
conceptions and outcomes of the Bezalel circles seemed to be hesitant and withdrawn
from the expression of a new society and a
new human being, a Hebrew on his soil.

Boris Schatz maintained distinct ties with
bourgeois Zionism in Europe, dictated by the
economic dependence of the school for the
crafts on zionist generosity; the output of the
workshops was intended for the buying
power of this Jewry, not only in Europe, but
also in the United States (in 1911-12, Bezalel
exhibited its products in London, Odessa,
Basel, and New York). The Bezalel style was
traditionally, ritualistically Jewish and, in this
sphere, it did not turn away from diaspora
Jewry and religion—the core of practical
Zionism and the essence of socialist Zionism.
This stand was taken by others, as well: the
absolute denial of the Diaspora and the
degrading and discriminatory history of the
Jewish people was already the main theme of
Jewish writers in Eastern Europe as early as
the middle of the Nineteenth century, from
Smolenskin and Berdichevsky, down to Yossef Haim Brenner, of the Second Aliya who,
in "Hapoel Hatzair," assailed the course of
Schatz and Bezalel.

The Bezalel style still had, traditional elements. Diasporic Jewish symbolism and traditional religious objects, commingled with
the influence of Jugendstil arabesque condi-
ments; plus distorted baroque and even neoclassical elements of the Eastern European heritage, which rendered it heavy and
unattractive. On the other hand, the Bezalel
style was a schematization of Palestinian,
Arab and Bedouin motifs, which would serve
to revive the spirit of the Bible and thereby
renew the ties with Hebrew existence in Eretz-
Israel, severed two thousand years earlier
when the Jewish people went into exile. The
renaissance of the Jewish people in its ances-
tral home meant its continued existence in the
East, bridging the two-thousand-year span in
exile. The renewal of these ties created the
term "Hebrew," applicable to the Jew who
returned to his homeland and struck root in
Eretz-Israel, the land of the Bible and of the

BEZALEL CLASS WITH ABEL PANN, 1913.

STUDENTS IN BEZALEL, 1913.

independence of ancient Israel.

The depiction of sites in Israel sanctified by Judaism was an important part of the Bezalel art repertoire in its first twenty years. This was a tangible and visual expression of the Jewish longing for redemption. Rachel's tomb near Bethlehem and the Western Wall were much in demand. Ira Yan, a young artist who came to Jerusalem after the Kishinev pogrom in 1905 and was close to Bezalel supporters, said at the time "there is nothing better than the Wall for painting the vision of revival." The figures of Zionist leaders, particularly the "prophet" image of Herzl, became popular subjects of Bezalel design.

Students who in the 1920s became the protagonists of the new art in Eretz-Israel, were castigated and even expelled because of their inclination toward deviation from academism, to what seemed to them to be Impressionism. One of these was Menahem Shemi. Paldi states that one of the acrimonious debates with the teachers in 1912 was over the question whether it was "permissible to paint a portrait in more than three colours." Rubin asked to engage in fine arts, but Schatz decreed for him a career in ivory carving. The students, it should be remembered, lived as a commune supported by the establishment. Expulsion from Bezalel, as a reaction to the move toward change, led to cancellation of such support, which meant, to all intents, that the student would have to

E.M. LILIEN, ABRAHAM AND ISAAC, 1909.

leave the country because of economic difficulties, and return to his parental home in Eastern Europe.

The acceptance of the images and styles of the Arab inhabitants as representative of the biblical Hebrews was, to the creators of the Bezalel style, a return to an authentic Hebrew style. However, the Zionist revolution, the daring socio-political avant-garde, was expressed by Bezalel in terms of an artistic retrograde. This was the crux of the failure of Boris Schatz and his group to create, at the beginning of the century, parallel with the Zionist settlement in Eretz-Israel and the denial of the Diasporic tradition, new, original, contemporary arts and crafts. The adherents of "implementation Zionism" naturally saw no connection betweem themselves and the Bezalel artists.

Most counterproductive to the expression of the new reality in Palestine, in the effulgence of its blinding sunshine, was the adherence of Schatz and his disciples to academic painting and their opposition to any innovative deviation, as well as to their obdurate stand regarding the momentous changes in art which began during the last decades of the Nineteenth Century. Significantly Bezalel was founded in the year of Cézanne's death, and also, in the first years of the activity of this Jerusalem institution, Europe formulated the Futurist Manifesto; Cubism, Abstractionism and the Russian Avant-garde turned Impressionism into a classical heritage, which was here rejected with unbelievable aggressiveness by Boris Schatz, even as he was attempting to create a new art for a new people.

True, Bezalel did become an intellectual centre and a social cynosure in Jerusalem, and Schatz did become a central figure in whatever pertained to design in the new community. In the planning for the first Hebrew high school, when the first Hebrew quarter, the harbinger of Tel-Aviv, was built on the sand dunes north of Jaffa in 1909, Schatz determined the façade of the eclectic structure—a combined image of a Russian palace, an Eastern fortress, a touch of the ancient wall of Jerusalem and the like; with reference also to the building of the tabernacle in the wilderness after the Israelite exodus from Egypt, in two stylized and serrated towers flanking the main entrance.

ABEL PANN, ILLUSTRATION OF THE BIBLE, 1920-1955.

LITHOGRAPHIC PRINTSHOP IN BEZALEL WITH ABEL PANN, 1921.

In his paintings, sculptures and bas-reliefs, Schatz reverts to exilic Jewish subjects from which his "implementation Zionism" followers sought to detach themselves. Lilien, who set the Bezalel style for many years, although he actually spent only one year there, transferred the Jugendstiel to Jerusalem, creating tortuous symbols and pseudo-Eastern illustration. Hirshenberg, in his paintings, symbolized the painful Diaspora. Abel Pann's lifetime dedication was to biblical

and exiled to Damascus for a year (Bezalel continued its existence under the supervision of the painter Aharon Shaul Schor). The school was assailed by extremist religious groups in Jerusalem, which regarded it as a centre of secularism and the source of permissiveness in the city. It was attacked even more acrimoniously by the socialist circles for "bringing the exile to Eretz-Israel" and alienating itself from pioneering Hebrew life. However, worldwide, Bezalel gained much

SHMUEL HARUBI, NEAR JERUSALEM, 1920's. WATERCOLOR.

works far from the reality in evocation; his models were the Arabs and the Bedouins.

The Bezalel style had no effect on Israeli art, and for a long time it remained only as a style in Eretz-Israel design. The Bezalel School for the Crafts existed until 1929, and its success lay in the establishment of workshops for practical crafts which continued under their own power and which long outlived the institution itself.

The obstacles which stood in the way of this school were tremendous. When the First World War broke out, the Turkish authorities became suspicious and even aggressive toward the institution. Schatz was arrested

renown among Jewish Zionist circles, symbolizing a nucleus of culture in Eretz-Israel, a conclusion that is borne out by many contemporary periodicals, among them "Die Welt" and "East and West."

Actually, Bezalel terminated its role with the advent of the mass immigration, following the First World War, of a young, pioneering, socialist and avant-garde generation. The young artists of this generation formed part of the new society which sought to begin afresh, with no obligations toward the Diaspora, like a revolt of children against parents. Palestine, captured by the British, became British mandated territory, and the Balfour

Declaration, expressing the right of the Jews to their national homeland, aroused hopes for a new future.

For the history of Israeli art, Bezalel, in its first fifteen years, formed the basis, the transitional stage from the Jewish Diaspora to the establishment of a new land, a necessary stage of purification which paved the way for the young art of the 1920s. The new political and social situations did away with the need for a school of the crafts.

Bezalel was a beginning, even though it has not affected art. As far as crafts are concerned, they also existed before Bezalel, but, in impoverished Jerusalem and Safed, in the Nineteenth Century, they consisted of ritualistic craftsmanship which had no connection with the concepts of Western art. The Bezalel crafts gave tangible meaning to a culture of spiritual-national identity, as was concluded in a study by the Israel Museum which brought to the surface an awareness of the existence of Jewish craftsmanship in Eretz-Israel in the Nineteenth Century. "The influence of the West on this craftmanship and Zionist settlement at the end of the century led to its decline." There is a basic fact relevant to art in Israel from its inception at the turn of the century: here art is bound to the West; this connection was not broken at any of the stages of its development, and it is currently becoming stronger.

The integration of the East in the Bezalel creativity was nothing more than an illustration, an unfulfilled desire, or an unrealized ideology. Here the East is always seen through Western eyes. This is true of the Eastern Hebrew mythos in the Jugendstiel graphic works of Ephraim Lilien and his successor Zeev Raban, and in the nostalgic Western biblical paintings by Abel Pann.

Schatz's artistic enterprise, met by opposition and isolation on the part of the formulators of the socialist society in the land and of the artists who set the image of the new art in the 1920s, was integrated in two important purposes of "implementation Zionism": the inculcation of the Hebrew language and the imposition of Hebrew labour. Schatz was a zealot when it came to Hebrew labour; he sought to create craftsmen in a native Hebrew style, from among Jews living in Eretz-Israel. Schatz, pushing for integration with the East, dressed in Eastern garb, stated, nevertheless as set forth in a letter from S. Ben-Zion to Ahad Ha'am: "The purpose of Bezalel is to create here a centre of artcrafts, by Jews. Anyone teaching Bezalel crafts to anyone but a Jew will be dismissed from the ranks of Bezalel instructors."

Chapter II

Art in an Idealistic Society: the Twenties

For the Jewish community in Palestine, as well as for the Zionist movement, the end of the First World War brought a tremendous historical turning point: the termination of the 400 year rule of the Ottoman Empire and, in its place, the protectorate of Great Britain. A large wave of immigration to Palestine began in 1919, mainly with the arrival of socialist Zionists, from Russia and other countries of Eastern Europe. The first ship to transport the immigrants was the Ruslan; it sailed from Odessa and anchored in Jaffa harbour in December 1919, and among its passengers were artists who became the designers of the new Israeli art. The Ruslan inaugurated the stage of intensive immigration which caused intensive settlement and the founding of kibbutzim. These rural communities formed the new cultural infrastructure, and to a large extent gave idealistic-socialistic character to Israeli society for many years. The waves of immigration in the 1920s increased the Jewish population by two and a half times, and the cultural centre moved from Jerusalem to Tel-Aviv, which had begun as a small sandy suburb of Jaffa and was now a European mini-metropolis in the heart of the Levant.

The impact of the new generation of artists crossed the borders of time. Some of them became identified as revolutionaries and stylistic innovators in Israeli art, even thirty years later. They were at home with the slogans of the October Revolution and the mottos of the Russian Avant-garde, and they sought to create a "new art for a new society." The atmosphere was a spur to physical creativity, with full awareness of its affinity to the making of history, the history of the people and the land. Every deed was measured in terms of "the upbuilding of the land," and so it

was with creativity in the arts, literature and the theatre. The recently arrived young people set up communes or formed socialist "labour battalions"—encampments of tents and shacks erected where there was hard work to be done, paving roads, quarrying, and draining swamps. Many of the artists and writers of this decade belonged to these "labour battalions." They settled accounts with Diasporic Jewish history, with their bourgeois homes in the cities and towns of Eastern Europe, and with the closed Jewish religion which, more than anything else, formed the image of the Diaspora Jew. They strove to prove, through their own person, the "normalization" and the "productivization" of the Jew as an individual and as a people, concepts repeatedly mentioned in the utterances of the first leaders and philosophers of Zionism at the beginning of the century. The new Jew was now a Hebrew, with his own soil and his own tongue, with an affinity to the culture and people of the ancient East, plus a socialist awareness. Such was the atmosphere at the beginning of the 1920s, the atmosphere of starting anew. The young artists felt they owed nothing either to the history of Diaspora Jewry or to the history of art, to the Zionist establishment in Europe, or to the purchasing power of bourgeois Jewry in the Diaspora; that is, to nothing of what Boris Schatz had to bear for his Bezalel enterprise in Jerusalem. This explains the rejection of Bezalel art by the young artists of the 1920s; it was part of their rejection of Old World Jewry. They sought to give expression to the physical reality of the new land, to its sun-flooded landscapes, to the concreteness of the new reality. The Arabs were to be held on a high pedestal because they were muscular natives, not because they were the models for biblical nostalgia, in the Bezalel style. Nahum Gutman, son of the writer S. Ben-Zion and a prototype of the artists of the 1920s who attended Bezalel in 1912, said: "We don't want to paint more old men at the Western Wall or marriage brokers with palm fronds. We see the Bible and its heroes not as wrinkled Yemenite Jews, but in the hillside crags, olive trees, the blue of the sea and the graceful movements of the Arabs around us."

The gradual shift of the central art activity from Jerusalem to Tel-Aviv also marked the gradual strengthening of the new pioneer spirit and the new generation of artists vis-à-vis the social and artistic conceptions of Bezalel which closed down in 1929 and was reopened, only after Boris Schatz's death, as the New Bezalel, in 1936. This was not, as is often assumed, a rebellion against Schatz and his group, but rather an accumulation of social, mental and political facts of a local nature, which undermined him. Jerusalem, in religious and historical wealth, could not compete with young Tel-Aviv, a town of white houses on the sand dunes, "the first all-Jewish city after two thousand years of exile." The new city was founded by 60 families in 1909; in 1925 it had 34,000 inhabitants. About 1000 *halutzim* (pioneers) settled the sand, and the writers and artists resident there numbered 133 (among them 41 women). It was a genuine centre for an artistic proletariat, a growing stronghold of the Labour Federation, for avant-garde periodicals and the first working-men's theatre, inaugurated in January of 1926 with the premiere exhibit of the works of modern artists.

The first steps toward the formation of an artists community and the mounting of art exhibits were taken in Jerusalem in 1920, as first proof of the enlightenment of the British regime in Palestine, headed by High Commissioner Sir Herbert Samuel (his being a Jew gave the small community high hopes for immediate independence, in the spirit of the Balfour Declaration in favour of the establishment of a "national home" in Eretz-Israel for the Jewish people). Under the aegis of District Governor Sir Ronald Storrs, the "Jerusalem Society" mounted an exhibit in the halls of David's Tower, the ancient fortress set into the Old City wall. This step led to the founding of the "Hebrew Artists Associa-

tion," which made its first appearance in April 1921. The period thence, till the last exhibition, in David's Tower in 1928, is known in Israeli art as the period of David's Tower. The next exhibition of the Hebrew Artists Association was held in Tel-Aviv. The exhibitions held there were the first to bring art to the people on a substantial scale. This was also the first expression of the establishmentarianism of art on the part of the British regime. Because the Bezalel School, with the instructors and graduates employed within its walls, was still the largest single reservoir of artists in Palestine—certainly in Jerusalem—the Hebrew Artists Association consisted mostly of Bezalel people. Henceforth we witness paintings done in accordance with nature, in a transitional academic-naturalistic manner, as with A.S. Schor; in an attempt to give expression to the sharp local illumination, as with Shmuel Haruvi; or with expressionistic proclivities as on the part of Levi-Ophel, who came from Bulgaria as a student with Boris Schatz in 1906. Here Abel Pann launched his lifetime work, over a span of forty years, painting and illuminating the Bible in a style which contained touches of Jugendstijl, leaning toward the romanticization of biblical myths in the images of local Arabs and Bedouins. In 1921 he went with Schatz to Vienna to bring in equipment for lithographic prints, and he began printing his lithographs on biblical subjects. Gur-Arye worked on silhouettes depicting pioneers and shepherds, contributing thereby to a "Hebrew" rather than a "Jewish" style of the later Bezalel period. It should also be mentioned that collaboration among the artists in the Bezalel workshops enabled them to create symbols and models (*Musterzeichner*) for the craftsmen, as stated in the first publication issued by Bezalel in 1906. Schatz, on the other hand, kept increasing the expression of traditional Judaism in his works, as he continued being carried on the wave of his nationalist utopia, with purposeful academistic and literary interpretation.

Schatz's determination to oppose change and the infiltration of modern concepts into his work or the Bezalel production in the 1920s is evident in his creations: pathetic images of the biblical prophets, such as Isaiah and Jeremiah, accompanied by Hebrew pas-

REUVEN RUBIN, JERUSALEM, c. 1923. COURTESY GORDON GALLERY, TEL-AVIV.

sages from the sources and fringed with baroque ornamentation, alongside types characteristic of Jewish life in the East European communities, like *The Marriage Broker,* plus the commemoration of religious rituals, such as *The Sabbath Candles.* His attitude was without doubt caused also by the growing evidence of a new kind of art developing in Eretz-Israel, created by young artists, in the picture mostly after 1919, who regarded themselves as part of a new society detached from exilic Jewry and who looked upon their creativity as part of the modern evolution going on in all of Europe's cultural centres. The first exhibition mounted by the Hebrew Artists Association in David's Tower already featured the work of Israel Paldi (Feldman), due to become one of the outstanding exponents of the new art in that very decade; of the sculptor Avraham Melnikof, about whom the young artists in Jerusalem gathered, after the First World War, and who was the first to make serious overtures to Assyrian and Sumerian sculpture as a possible source for the new Eretz-Israeli art; and of

the painter Levine, described by his contemporaries as "the first of the modernists" who told them about the existence of works by Cézanne. Levine died early in the 1920s, leaving not a single specimen of his work; several artists who worked here in that early period of Israeli art also left nothing of their creativity. In this David's Tower exhibition, in 1920, arts and crafts were still exhibited together, since crafts were regarded as being of primary importance both for the creation of a national style and for the school's achievement in training Jews in new productive and aesthetic vocations.

Indeed, in the early 1920's there were 365 smiths, ivory carvers, olive wood fashioners, and photographers in Jerusalem (the Bezalel photography studio was definitely a major innovation in Jerusalem's artisan community). Furthermore, the by-laws of the Hebrew Artists Association, formulated in 1920, declared that "the aim of the Association is to develop and disseminate among the people the values of humanism and art, in good state and in the Hebrew spirit."

Artistic and crafts activity in Jerusalem accelerated, and the school's budget now came from the Zionist Organization which, until 1926, recognized Bezalel as a national institution. Bezalel trainees set up independent workshops for casting sculptures, weaving carpets, silversmithing, and lithography. The halls of the school were always taken up with exhibitions by Schatz and Abel Pann; the museum, which later formed the nucleus of the Israel Museum, was not opened until 1925. Every building in the city seemed to be exhibiting. In 1922 the Association mounted an exhibition in the home of a Zionist stalwart, Dr. Eader. The first one-man show, comprised of about 100 paintings by Joseph Tepper, a new settler in Jerusalem, was displayed at David's Tower. He was followed immediately by Abel Pann who mounted a comprehensive display which included his paintings for the Book of Genesis.

The exhibition which marked the turning point and the beginning of Israeli art in Jerusalem was the one-man show of Israel Paldi, held at the Lemel School, in April of 1923. The beginning of Eretz-Israeli art in Tel-Aviv had already been marked in 1920, with the founding of a cooperative by young artists who arrived aboard the Ruslan, from Odessa. In Jerusalem the turning point was the Paldi exhibit, and it was only in January of 1926 that the entire activity of modern art filtered down to Tel-Aviv.

Reviewing the formation of this art in Jerusalem before going on to its new development in Tel-Aviv, we find the period before 1929 characterized by the activity of the Bezalel School, centre, and workshops; the mounting of exhibitions at David's Tower by the Hebrew Artists Association, and the innovative mountings of one-man shows by young artists on public premises, schools and clubs. The few means of communication, in the form of the daily newspapers ("Doar Hayyom" and "Ha'aretz" were added in 1919) and weeklies (among them Brenner's "Adamah") carried odd critiques which repeatedly evaluated the paintings in the light of their interpretation of the society and the land.

Paldi, dismissed from Bezalel together with Menahem Shemi (Schmidt) because of his demand that the curriculum be modernized, returned to Jerusalem in 1920 after a period of study at the Munich Academy. He painted static, massive works, reflecting expressionism, on one hand, and a dull absorption of cubism, on the other. "There was little that was soft in my paintings," he said. "Perhaps because of the impact of a harsh environment. We young artists were of the same spirit as the socialist Aliya immigration, who arrived in Palestine from 1919 to 1924. We lived in the illusion of creating a new society." The author and journalist Avigdor Hameiri said about Paldi's exhibition, "Something new is evolving here." And he was right. This statement reappeared, in the first half of the 1920s, in many articles, and not only with reference to art. Anticipation of the new and a receptive attitude toward new experiments went along with the feeling of history-in-the-making. But the receptiveness was there only to the extent that the work gave expression to the new land and to the aims of its society. Already in 1922, one of the five newspapers appearing in Palestine which published critiques from time to time, wrote: "For Paldi, the lines in the landscape and the lines of the machine are too harsh to become blurred, particularly here in the East, where

ISRAEL PALDI, THE FAMILY, 1924.

21

the contours are more visible, due to the strong sunlight." Paldi did much painting of Arab stevedores at the Jaffa port, as a depiction of a typical human scene, using these figures models of the working man—muscular, down to earth and part of it.

In 1924 there were unmistakable signs of a new Eretz-Israeli art, of the emergence a group of young artists, and even of "cultural stars" in the firmament of plastic art in Palestine: Yossef Zaritsky and Reuven Rubin mounted their first exhibition, and that year's David's Tower show consisted mostly of young artists who had arrived during the last four years with the Zionist-socialist wave of immigrants. This event, as well as their next exhibit, in January 1926 in the hut of the Ohel Workers' Theatre in Tel-Aviv (more about this exhibition later), finalized the command over Eretz-Israeli art and the emergence of a "modern" local style.

Most of these artists were born in the last decade of the Nineteenth Century: Zaritsky, Menahem Shemi, Litwinovsky, Yitzhak Frenkel, Uri Zivoni, in the Ukraine; Israel Paldi, in Russia; and Reuven Rubin, Melnikof and Nahum Gutman, in Rumania. Ziona Tajar was born in Jaffa, and Arye Lubin grew up in Chicago. The other artists who worked with them in the 1920's—Hayim Glicksberg, Arye Alweil, Shmuel Ovadyahu and Baruch Agadati—were also born in Eastern Europe, in the 1890s.

The conception characteristic of Eretz-Israeli painting in the 1920s, which featured massiveness and/or naïveté and primitiveness, was a matter of choice rather than unfamiliarity. "The artists," said Oigen Kolb, curator of the Tel-Aviv Museum in the early 1950s, "detach themselves from anything which looks to them to be a thing of the past." Here there was no tradition of painting, no directive authority. No museums and no professional critique. They themselves, most of them in their twenties, had to set norms, to initiate tradition. And they knew it.

Reuven Rubin's paintings in 1922 depicted Tel-Aviv and Jerusalem with a naïveté and a hand that "began with genesis," alternately with a massiveness which brings to

NAHUM GUTMAN, JAFFA ORANGE GROVES, 1926.

mind the works of Henri Rousseau. Rubin had exhibited, a year earlier, in the Anderson Gallery in New York under Stieglitz's aegis, and in such company as George Martin, Georgia O'Keefe, Hartley and Dove. A year later he said: "Rumania I had forgotten. New York was very far away. In Eretz-Israel the sun was shining, there was the sea, there were the pioneers and their tanned bodies, faces bronzed and shirts open. A new land and a new life were rising around me. I put aside everything I knew. The world around me became clear and pure. Life was primordial, denuded, primitive." His earlier paintings, dominated by Hodler's influence, gave way to unrecognizable change.

In 1926, in an exhibit by modern artists in Tel-Aviv, Yitzhak Frenkel displayed a non-objective composition, the first of its kind to be seen in Palestine. Immediately afterwards he turned his back on this style and went over to expressionist painting. Arie Lubin, a graduate of the Chicago Academy, displayed in the same exhibition the paintings he had executed in Tel-Aviv in 1924: cubist abstractions with a touch of still life. From this style he switched at once to Cézanne-like landscapes, and thence to a style of Eastern folklore-like figures which he was still painting fifty years later.

Ziona Tajar returned from Paris, where she had been studying with André L'Hote. Nahum Gutman came back to Tel-Aviv at the end of 1925 after a five-year stay in Berlin, Vienna and Paris. Since then, and over a period of many years, he fostered in his paintings two parallel myths: the myth of Hebrew Tel-Aviv, rising on the sands on the Jaffa boundary line, and the myth of the Palestinian Arab, or, to put it another way, the myth of the pioneering society clutching at the dunes and at the soil of the land, and the myth of the land relevant to its original inhabitants. From his early childhood, Gutman grew up in the first Hebrew quarter outside Jaffa, and as the son of S. Ben-Zion, editor of "Haomer," his environment was peopled by Jewish intellectuals, among them Shai Agnon who, half a century later, was to win the Nobel Prize in Literature for his books on the saga of the new, pre-Tel-Avivian settlement. The circles around Gutman were those of the first Hebrew writers in Eretz-Israel, and the con-

AVRAHAM MELNIKOF, EGYPTIAN ARAB, 1925.
REINFORCED CONCRETE.

tention about the essence of the literature paralleled the controversy on the essence of art in the beginning of the century. Gutman maintained an ambivalence, one of the elements of which was the rejection, although not stated, of the Odessa circles and of Ahad Ha'am and the Hebrew "poet laureate" Bialik—his father's close friend.

Gutman's complete concentration, in the 1920s, on the depiction of the Arab and his surroundings and on the Levantinê-Palestinian life style is a juxtaposition of the natural and creative native against the protagonists of the East European Jewish traditions, which carried over to the new land in the works of the early writers in Hebrew, at the turn of the century.

Gutman lived and studied in Vienna and Berlin from 1920 to 1924. There, too, he was in the company of Hebrew writers. He drew illustrations for Bialik's work on Jewish legends, and studied engraving with Hermann Struck, who was also the mentor of Uri Lesser, Chagall, and Steinhardt. (Struck settled in Palestine and created bright engravings, under the impact of local effulgence, but his works had no impact on his contem-

23

NAHUM GUTMAN, MIDDAY REPOSE, 1926. COLLECTION D. GUTMAN.

poraries).

Nahum Gutman's creativity in Palestine, as of the end of 1925, derives from the tenets of the art he witnessed in Paris, just before his return to Tel-Aviv, characteristic of the new art he found here, in painting: almost monumentally static, an exaggerated weight of shapes and forms in the landscape, an emphasis on circumferential lines, preference for voluminous structures, a kind of paraphrase of taking hold of site, a bond with the soil, with antiquity, entrenchment rather than soaring in space, rootedness instead of the Jew's eternal wandering. Picasso's paintings of 1920, the return to the classical, responded to Gutman's quests and to searchings of other contemporaries, such as Menahem Schmidt, for massiveness, earthiness and rootedness.

It is interesting to compare Gutman's *Midday Repose,* painted immediately after his return in 1925, with Picasso's *Sleeping Peasants* of 1919. Gutman's sleeping peasant is an Arab; the watermelon and the knife stuck into it are site markers—the haystacks

and the contour of the hillocks, the sensuous thighs of an Arab peasant woman.

The problem confronting Gutman, Rubin, and others, centred on integrating massiveness with uplifted spirituality, with optimism carried along toward poetry and sentiment. To them, the static and naïve in the paintings of Henri Rousseau appeared to be possible avenues of expression. Many of Rubin's works are reminders of this artist's approach. In a short span of time, Gutman became completely dedicated to the depiction of the charms of the East. In his writings about this epoch, we find descriptions suited to his works of the 1920s: "His ears caught the staccato vibration of the silver bells around the horses' necks; he saw the back of the Arab coachman, robed in a shiny silk shirt and wide trousers. Up ahead, ostrich feathers stuck into the horses' manes waved gently. His diligence moved along through the incense aroma of coffee. He was wafted into a legend of the East. He had several poems on longing for the East, but until now he had no idea of the tastes, scents and sensualities those poems espoused. He had no idea that daily life can have colours, scents and shapes, capable of overcasting everything conceived in the mind and the brain."

This romantic enthusiasm was a far cry from Jewish life in Eastern Europe, and it was the expression of revolt against the paternal generation. Rubin, too, in the mid-1920s, shifted from the massive to the Oriental and to representing an overcast poetic reality.

Gutman saw the mysterious in the East as impenetrable and unintegrated: "The big red gate was always locked and shut off our view of the green world bordering the sand dunes of Tel-Aviv. We saw the orange grove as if it were a chapter taken from the legends of *A Thousand and One Nights*." I am emphasizing this point because it coincided with the duality of Eretz-Israeli society in the period of its settling in Palestine—and not only then. The political declarations about "the building of a common future in partnership with the Arabs in the land" were made in the face of violent struggle for the right to the land, a struggle which has not been decided to this very day. It should be kept in mind that at every stage the society and culture of the Eretz-Israel was Western, as were the quality of life and the environment. When the founders of Tel-Aviv, in 1909, decided upon their pioneering move, they declared: "We intend to create a new city not only so as to build good and pretty homes, but also to improve the life style and etiquette, which can be done only if we detach ourselves from Jaffa. We shall ... build our city neither within its confines nor in its life style. We must assume all the hardships imposed upon us, so long as there will be distance between us and Jaffa." I make note of this in order to stress the schizophrenia between viewing the Arab as the ideal new individual and actual reality.

Another possible affinity to the East in the works of the generation of artists in the 1920s is found in Avraham Melnikof, one of the outstanding members of the group. Melnikof turned to the culture of the ancient East in an attempt to create original sculpture. The sculpture of the lion he erected at Tel-Hai, in memory of those who fell in the defense of this small pioneer Jewish outpost against the attacking Galilean Arabs, was built in 1926 but was dedicated only in 1934, after a public outcry caused by the contention that the sculpture did not represent the valour of the

AVRAHAM MELNIKOF, THE LION OF TEL HAI, 1926. UNDER CONSTRUCTION.

AVRAHAM MELNIKOF, THE LION OF TEL HAI, 1926-34.

25

ELIAHU SIGARD, LANDSCAPE WITH SHEPHERDS, 1929. WATERCOLOR.

fighters. It was dedicated only after a committee, headed by Bialik, confirmed its objective. Melnikof went to England and never returned to Palestine as an artist.

We have noted the first appearance of Yossef Zaritsky in a 1924 exhibit in Jerusalem, a year after his arrival from Russia. His prominence in the artists community went unquestioned for many decades. His creations marked another possibility for Eretz-Israeli painting in the early stage; he was the one who turned this art, at the end of the 1940s, in the direction of abstractionism. He was not bound to the system of visual representation which strove to create an identity of the work with the return to the homeland, with the affinity to the East, the earthiness and the massive. He kept away from the expressionism which also characterized the 1920s and the 1930s. His post-impressionistic approach was already set in his first paintings in Palestine, displayed in his 1924 exhibit in Jerusalem. In his aquarels—his exclusive medium for over twenty years—his view of reality is decidedly Cézanne-like. Colourful, contourless marks, airiness of background, and changes of direction at the touch of the

brush—these were the instruments which served him in his painting of the Eretz-Israeli landscape. He objected to localism and to the preference for subjects which seemed to coincide with the moods of the idealistic society. To him, the presentation of light was expressive of the site, and he depicted this relation without recourse to symbolism.

When Zaritsky reached Palestine he was already a mature painter. He showed signs of the influence of Mikhail Vroubel, a student of Repine. His free colourful system of marks led Zaritsky, at the end of the 1940s, toward abstractionism. His artistic and organizational authority was patent in all the progressions in the formation of local modern art. Without being identified with the aspirations espoused by the society about him, his acceptance by the artists and the establishment was without question.

Zaritsky's exhibition in Jerusalem came at a time of unprecedented cultural revival in the city. European artists came there to paint (among them Leonid Pasternak, father of the author of *Dr. Zhivago*). The central figure in Hebrew poetry, Chaim Nahman Bialik, took up permanent residence in Eretz-Israel, and a year later the Hebrew University opened its doors on Mount Scopus.

For our purposes, as mentioned above, the exhibition by modern artists in January of 1926 in Tel-Aviv marked the crystallization of Eretz-Israeli art and of Tel-Aviv as the centre of art in Palestine. This phenomenon calls for a survey of cultural development in Tel-Aviv. Unlike Jerusalem, Tel-Aviv was open to innovation and new trends, and curious about the development of a socialist culture, mingled with the bourgeois atmosphere engendered by the Fourth Aliya, mainly form Poland, which turned the settlement into a city.

Among the thousand immigrants who arrived from Odessa aboard the Ruslan in 1919, were artists whose names are intertwined with the process of converting Tel-Aviv into an art centre; among them were Yitzhak Frenkel, Constant, and Had Gadya. Another passenger aboard the Ruslan was the collector and public figure Jacob Peremen. This combination led to the founding of an artists cooperative in Jaffa, Hatomer, the first of its kind, with the support of the socialist "Hapoel Hatzair." This support was in line with the ideology of the movement and its aims to involve the Hebrew worker in all spheres of labour (artistic creativity was regarded as labour in the definition of the movement). The Hatomer cooperative sought to create a modern art centre in Tel-Aviv and to offer art and craft services to the small community, which was in no desperate need of them. The cooperative did not exist long, but the exibition of its members' works, in the halls of the Herzlia High School, was a festive event in the experience of the tiny local art centre. In her research, Gila Balas, commenting on Hatomer and Peremen's activities, notes that Constant was already working and displaying his cubistic works. Moreover, Peremen had brought with him a collection of modern works by Jewish artists in Russia. While these artists were not widely known, some (like Malik) worked under the influence of Gauguin, and others (like Sobol and Nou-

ISRAEL PALDI, LANDSCAPE, 1928. OIL ON CANVAS. COLLECTION ISRAEL MUSEUM.

YOSSEF CONSTANT, A YEMENITE, 1920.
CHARCOAL DRAWING.

BARUCH AGADATI DANCES,
TEL-AVIV, 1924.

renberg) in a somewhat cubist style. Peremen, founder, in Odessa, of the Eretz-Israel League for the Promotion of Art, which was designed to establish a centre for Jewish artists in the spirit of Zionism, sought to fill the function, in Eretz-Israel, of Chtehoukine. For three years, beginning in 1920, he exhibited his collection, the likes of which had never before been seen in the land. The exhibits, mounted in Tel-Aviv, included works by members of Hatomer and, later, by others. The showings, in the framework of The Palestine Permanent Art Gallery, also offered catalogues containing a national modern manifesto which said, "The most suitable path to creativity is the synthesis of the past and the future. The artist is, first and foremost, a son of his people and his land, and he cannot divest himself of the romantic and educational sentiments in his people's development."

Aboard the Ruslan, which now appears to have been a "cultural Mayflower," also came Baruch Agadati, creator of the concept of "Hebrew dance." Agadati, a Bezalel student from 1910, returned to Odessa, and during the First World War he became a ballet dancer in the municipal troupe as a solo performer with Bronislawa Nijinska, the sister of the Russian ballet maestro. While in Odessa, Agadati was steeped in the environment in which the avant-garde of dance fluorished. In 1920, in a building set on the sand dunes of Tel-Aviv, Agadati appeared in a new type of dance which integrated the new concepts with the Hassidic Jewish tradition. He declared his intention of creating a Hebrew dance, and fused the lessons he had learned from Isadora Duncan and the Russian Avant-garde into Hassidic and Yemenite dances, in the strangest style yet seen. Agadati designed the costumes together with the young artist Litwinovsky, showing a predominance of cubistic conception. In his recitals Agadati adopted the music of Bartoky, bringing to Tel-Aviv an atmosphere of innovation and a mood of ferment. He took ballets he created here (always for solo performers) to Paris, and in 1924 he appeared on the Paris stage. His costumes were designed by Gontcharova and Laryonov, in what is perhaps the only known direct contact of an Israeli artist with the creators of the Russian Avant-garde.

In Tel-Aviv, Agadati created mass happenings by getting the people into the streets for events of activity. In 1929 he issued a statement, together with the author Avigdor

Hameiri, in which he declared: "Let us say it immediately and forthrightly. Our desire is not to show something to the people, but on the contrary, to let the public see itself. The public is the creator. We don't want a performance, but real life!"

Avant-garde Hebrew dance did not last, but Agadati was the first to set up a film studio, in a Tel-Aviv hut, and from the '30s on he created aquarels on silk, in the manner of Persian design.

The elements of the Russian Avant-garde brought to Tel-Aviv by Agadati in 1920 received special impetus with the founding of the labour theatre, Ohel, in a shack facing the sea. This theatre, or as it was called, "The Drama Studio of the Hebrew Labourers Federation," was founded in days of economic hardship and mounting unemployment—in the same days that Tel-Aviv became a European city on the Mediterranean seashore, with white villas and private mansion-like homes in a surprisingly eclectic style, coffee shops, and an opera house (launched in 1923 with a performance of *Rigoletto*). The theatre hut was opened with an exhibition by "modern artists," even before it offered a première performance. The sponsorship of an art show by the theatre created a short-lived impression of a cultural force which was shaping the image of the new society, of an artistic proletarian brotherhood. Slogans of the Russian Avant-garde and the sentiments of the October Revolution affected the exhibition and the preparations to launch the labour theatre. Mayakovsky's appeal—"Let us convert the streets into brushes and the squares into palettes"—did not sound odd alongside declarations concerning the roots of Hebrew art. The catalogue of the *Modern Artists* exhibition of January 1926 opens with a manifesto, written by the creator of the Ohel, the stage director Moshe Halevi, which furnishes a clear indication of the moods and concepts of culture in Tel-Aviv, in the mid-1920s: "Eretz-Israel is the Israeli concentration point: territorially and spiritually. Gradually the forces of Hebrew creativity, in all its manifestations, are gathering here. A new will, experiments and quests are being woven here."

Ohel strove to heal the schism between the various kinds of artistry and to close the rifts within each of them. Its aim was to prevent the alienation of the public from the creative work. Ohel attempted to create a single cyno-

YOSSEF ZARITSKY, NACHLAT SHIV'A, JERUSALEM 1924. PENCIL AND WATERCOLOR.

MENAHEM SHEMI (SCHMIDT), THE ARTIST'S WIFE WITH CAT, 1928.
COLLECTION HAIFA MUSEUM OF MODERN ART.

URI ZIV'ONI, ON THE BEACH OF TEL-AVIV, 1924.

sure of concentration and cooperation, of all types of creativity, in one overall expression of "the theatre of the masses" (the stage of the people).

This exhibition was part and parcel of the activities engendered by Ohel to realize its aims. At that time many Hebrew artists of various backgrounds and intents were in Eretz-Israel, and the need was felt to totalize their separate searchings, as well as to fuse activity in the visual arts with the other manifestations of creativity. There was a need for a platform which would talk in the language of colours to the masses, not to a small circle of initiates. From this viewpoint, this was a première exhibition in Eretz-Israel. Speeches were held at the opening whose content I found in the pages of a yellowing notebook in the archives of Yehuda Gabbai, one of the pioneers of the labourers theatre. These speeches occasion a rare opportunity for understanding the problem of art in that period. Abraham Shlonsky, a recent arrival, at once became one of the most prominent figures, as the poet of,"progressive culture," a socialist who brought to Tel-Aviv the culture of the revolution. He assailed the conservatives, also castigating the religious circles in a struggle to influence the image of the society (a struggle he carried over in due time to the State of Israel): "God is gone, never to return! I propose a surrogate as a substitute for God: the exhibition in Ohel. We must have there a new synagogue, that is, we should replace God. The liturgist should be in the painter's

circle and the painter in the musician's circle. Ohel will serve us as a substitute for God and as a synagogue of art."

Avigdor Hameiri, a prominent poet and publicist, said on the same occasion: "The misunderstanding we find here is due to the fact that we have become a European people, something we have not felt during the two thousand years of exile. We are ambivalent: on the one hand we wish to preserve that which is inherent in our people, and on the other to tear down the gates and penetrate into European progressiveness. How can we bridge the two trends? The battle between conservatism and progress is a war to the end. We are faced with a parodox—how is bourgeois Zionism to support the working class and its future development? The collective type being created here, and the psychology attending this process, is something entirely new. If we can express this art, to give espression to labour and labourers as the ideal of the collective, then we shall reach an achievement greater than socialism—we shall reach the level of the Prophets. Ohel should assume responsibility for Jewry and for the development of art. It must create a large stage for creativity, so as to attain to an inner understanding which would point the way to the preservation of the existent and to opening the gates for world progress."

About plastic arts, it is worth quoting the painter Israel Paldi: "To me, the modern Hebrew painting is necessary and vital. We have no painting tradition. During the

EXHIBITION OF MODERN ARTISTS IN THE OHEL THEATRE, TEL-AVIV, 1926.
IN THE CENTER AN ABSTRACT PAINTING BY YITZHAK FRENKEL.

SHMUEL SHLESINGER, WOMAN ON SOFA, 1922.

Emancipation we merely followed others, conservatives or revolutionaries. Now our painting must become part of modern art.

"We get special gratification as we look at machinery. The traffic flowing in the streets is attended by artificial lighting and gives rise to new thoughts about light waves. The laws of the new technology are changing our concept of the beautiful and have an impact on modern creativity. The laws of light and shadow in the paintings of Leonardo da Vinci are replaced by new dynamics, and the variegation in current life is far from the tranquil rural life of that period. Also, the modern artist must be simple, since the piling up of details in the age of the cinema is a ridiculous procedure."

The feeling was that history was being made, that life was a mission—yet at that time, as the old-timers living in our midst say, the artists were going hungry, as were so many others in their milieu.

In the ideal society, the acts of the individual are measured in accordance with his affinity to the ideals; so was the critique of the *Modern Artists* exhibition gauged by the affinity of the artworks to the society and the labouring community. The criterion for the

critique of the work was its adherence to "the ideal now in progress, the ideal of labour in Eretz-Israel." Reuven Rubin's paintings were appraised negatively because "his envisioning of events is almost religious. Everything is tranquil with him, or it sees visions. And what truck do we have with that pure, almost bleached, religious attitude? His regard is of holiday colours and festival attire. And we haven't rested even a single Sabbath—we, the builders of the Tiberias roads and the hewers of Jerusalem stone." The conclusion brings us even closer to the sense of life in that period: "No, Reuven Rubin's place is not here just as the site of concrete works is not the place for a book of lyric poetry." Yitzhak Frenkel's non-objective paintings received an open critique: "His constructivist compositions are an entirely new manifestation in the land." The critic compared the phenomenon of the paintings to the first appearance of the machine in Palestine. Frenkel at once abandoned the abstract approach, although in 1927 it was still said that "he adheres to the essential to the point of abstraction." During his lengthy sojourn in Paris (1920-1925, 1926-1934) he came closer to the Jewish expressionist artists—Soutine, Kremegne, Kikoïne, Max

32

Band—and became one of the more important influences on the general shift of art in Eretz-Israel toward this expressionism. Frenkel headed the first significant studio for painters, opened in Tel-Aviv in 1925 by the Histadrut-Labour Federation, which "proclaimed itself as the bearer of the socialist idea in painting," a definition found in the contemporary press, although there was no expression of this in the works of Frenkel or of his disciples in those days—Mordechai Levanon, Holzmann, David Hendler, and others.

Modern artists' exhibitions were held in the Ohel hut until 1928. Among the participants was Elweil, who came in 1920 as a pioneer, went to Vienna to study, exhibited in Paris, and returned to Eretz-Israel in 1926. Prior to his return he painted in a cubist fashion, but on his arrival he turned what we have called genetic Eretz-Israeli painting—naïve and massive. Litwinovsky and Hayim Gliksberg (the latter an intimist and expressionist), took part in this exhibit as they had in the David's Tower shows. Yoel Tanneanbaum and Shmuel Schlesinger Zellinger exhibited in Jerusalem, in this framework, but although they were to paint many years thereafter (Schlesinger is a member of the Ein-Hod artists colony), they and their paintings were almost forgotten.

The sculptor Hanna Orloff was a visitor to Tel-Aviv in those days. In Paris she had been a popular figure in Jewish artists' circles, and here she fell in with the modern artists. The works of Max Band, also a Parisian, were displayed in a group exhibition mounted by the Hebrew Artists Association in Jerusalem, in 1926. Another participant in that show in Palestine, for the first time, was the artist and architect Leopold Krakauer from Vienna, the harbinger of the German Jewish artists who made an impression on Jerusalem in the 1930s. Batya Lishansky, a Bezalel product, exhibited expressionistic wooden figures, in Jerusalem, drawing on her experience in Berlin. In 1929 she began work on the construction of a heroic stone monument in Kibbutz Hulda.

In striving to integrate the arts the Ohel workers theatre did not function in a vacuum. The excitement engendered by the effort was tremendous, considering that the Jewish population of Tel-Aviv, in the mid-1920s, was but some 25,000 souls. "Davar," the daily newspaper of the Eretz-Israel Labour Party, made its appearance in 1925, as did the first issue of "Theatre and Art." That year Gabirel Talpir arrived, and in 1927 he published a volume of his dadaist poems, *Jazz Band* and

ARIE LUBIN, NARGHILEH SMOKERS, 1950.

ZIONA TAJAR, KALMAN FROM Y.L. PERETZ PLAY,
IN THE OHEL THEATRE, 1927.
COLLECTION JOSEPH HACKMEY, TEL-AVIV.

ARIE LUBIN, STILL LIFE, 1924.

the manifesto *Zrom (Flow)*. Later, in 1932, he launched the publication of "Gazit," a periodical of art and literature, which became an indispensable source of information about the development of art in Eretz-Israel.

The first piece to be performed by Ohel was Y.L. Peretz's work (beyond the avant-garde and socialist Hebrew battle cries—an attachment to the sources of culture and Judaism in the Diaspora). Demonstrations by the unemployed were becoming more frequent, in concomitance with the carnivals and happenings organized by the avant-garde dancer Baruch Agadati on his return to Palestine from Paris.

The founding of Ohel was preceded by Hebrew drama circles set up even before the establishment of Tel-Aviv. In 1904 performances were held in Jaffa by the Society of Friends of the Dramatic Arts, and in 1919, members of Hapoel Hatzair put on Chekhov's Bear. Another troupe performed Ibsen's *Spirits*—in Hebrew, of course, as no one would sanction the performance of a play in any other language. It was not until 1920 that Tel-Aviv had a professional theatre, the Hebrew Theatre of Eretz-Israel, presenting Chekhov in the main; with the actors living in a commune. Five years later the Eretz-Israel Theatre come into being, with a stage director, with costuming first by Rubin and later, for the performance of the *Dybbuk*, by Litwinovsky. The music was also "Hebrew," composed by Yoel Engel.

The pride of the Hebrew theatre, Habimah was founded in Moscow in 1918 as one of the studios attached to the theatre managed by Stanislavsky. Its establishment came from the avowed intent of the Russian Revolution to foster the culture of the national minorities. Habimah visited Palestine for the first time early in 1926. Menahem Shemi designed the costumes for Calderon de la Barca's *David's Crown*; in Moscow, costumers for Habimah included Robert Falk and Nathan Altman, who designed the costumes, in 1922 for the *Dybbuk*. In 1931 Habimah took up permanent residence in Tel-Aviv, and after the inception of the State of Israel, it became the Israel National Theatre.

The art created in Palestine in the 1920s ertainly laid the groundwork for the art

NATHAN ALTMAN, STAGE FOR THE DYBBUK, HABIMA THEATRE, 1922.

created in Eretz-Israel, and it bore (or indicated) the problems of an idealist society striking root in a new land. That this art declined from engaging in the problems of art for its own sake and refrained from being carried away by the new and exciting currents arising in Europe in that decade, could not have been a result of detachment alone. We have already seen in detail that most of the young artists who came to Palestine during this decade had already taught in academies or had spent time in European art centres; and the trips to Paris of the senior artists were by no means rare. The main reason for their engaging in a search for original local art was that, being part of an idealistic society, they regarded every act as part of a social or national effort. The expression of their communion with the land, the "conquest" of its scope and essence, were of greater moment than one interpretation or another of a new conception of European Avant-garde art. The problems of the local society, the difficult existence, and the very decision of the artist to live in Eretz-Israel, contrary to every artistic ego, were part of the concession inherent in the choice, at the expense of art and in favour

of Zionism. Even those who tried, like Yitzhak Frenkel in abstractionism and in *Dynamic Rhythms in Space*, and Arie Lubin in cubism, retreated to the local descriptive painting. Even Menahem Shemi, in his quick transitions from the characteristic massive-local to landscape depictions with cubist volume, concluded, "I am convinced that emotionally, in all of my conceptions of life and art, I am close to the artists who created an atmosphere in their localities." Only Yossef Zaritsky went on his consistent course of Postimpressionism; at the end of the 1940s, this was to lead him to abrsactionism.

To the artists of the 1920s, "new art for a new society" meant art for a society that rebelled against its history. The "innovation" for these artists was the turning away from national traditions, not a rebellion against implied artistic tradition, which is meaningless in the context of social and personal redemption— the framework of pioneering Zionist settlement in Eretz-Israel. John Graham points out in the *System and Dialectics of Art* (1937) that revolution is possible only where there is tradition. No tradition—no revolution. In Eretz-Israel, tradition was a national matter.

35

The new painting responded to national queries by virtue of its very existence.

The dominance of Jewish Parisian expressionism, from the end of the 1920s onward encountered no serious opposition in Eretz-Israel. The process seemed quite natural with the end of the first years of reaction to the experience of the encounter with the land and its Levantinism. The naïveté and the enthusiasm faded gradually. The urban centres kept growing, and Tel-Aviv with its casino on the beach, and Berlin-style cafés, with the fashions in the early 1930s of the petit-bourgeoise immigrants from Europe, and the Hebrew settlements merging with the landscape—all appeared to be very distant from the depicted image of the Arab as the ideal to be exalted. The bloody assaults by the Arabs and their violent objection to a Jewish community in Palestine, demonstrated in the unprecedented riots in the summer of 1929, led to deep disillusionment regarding the possibility of coexistence.

French art, as a source to be drawn upon, did not run counter to the cultural affinity of Zionist society in Eretz-Israel, which regarded itself from its very inceptions as a Western society, striving for sovereign independence and for acceptance as an equal

YITZHAK FRENKEL, THE SACRIFICE OF ISAAC, 1930's.

among equals in the European community of nations. Only later, in the early 1940s with the outbreak of the Second World War, the rise of anti-semitism and Nazism, and the exile of Jews from Europe, did young artists in Israel look for roots to hold on to in the ancient historical homeland of the Hebrew nation, also seeking connection and continuity in the culture of the ancient East, in the family of the semitic nations, the Canaanites, the Sumerians and the Assyrians.

ARIE ELWEIL, DONKEYS, c. 1930.
COLLECTION ISRAEL ARGAMAN.

Chapter III

The Era
of Expressionism

Already in 1926, with Yitzhak Frenkel's return from Paris and the formation of a circle of young artists around his studio in Tel-Aviv, expressionist painting was making its presence known. Young artists who, in the decade to come, were to become the protagonists of Eretz-Israeli Expressionsim, like Mordechai Levanon, Aharon Avni, Holzman, Kossonogi, and Zvi Schor, were being nurtured in Expressionism in line with the interpretation by Frenkel and other artists who were leaving the beaten track of the styled localism known to us as the early Eretz-Israeli style. Young men like Yehezkel Streichman, Stematsky and Aroch, who twenty years afterwords were to initiate the move toward abstractionism, were in those years the acolytes of Expressionism.

Tel-Aviv art circles, dedicated to social idealism, were split toward the end of the 1920s, with regard to the expressionist trends, which seemed to be turning away from the quest for original style. An article in Ha'aretz on the problems of modern painting intimated a trend toward liberation from nationalistic obligations: "It would be of much advantage to the development of the Jewish artists in the land, if they were to feel less obliged to be the expression of their people's spirituality. The painters working and creating in Eretz-Israel, the centre of Hebrew renascence, will find there a public which does not ask whether their work is of Jewish content. It is important, as well, not to exert pressure on the artist to be proletarian in his work, and to allow him freedom of creativity." This was something new, but, on the other hand, already in 1927 there was vociferous criticism: "We regard the *Modern Artists* exhibition as a negative influence of Expres-

sionism and its Parisian source."

The Eretz-Israeli artists were bent upon finding an egress from the massive naïveté which characterized the beginning of this decade in local art. In their landscapes they sought to find an affinity to the locale, not only subject-wise but also as an emotional reaction intended to transmit the experience of the identity with the place. Nahum Gutman described the bond between young people, coming from a variety of countries, as a common experience of landscape painting when he was still a student at Bezalel, before the First World War. The description of the landscapes and the characteristic local effulgent light became, in the 1930s, a kind of singular test of the Eretz-Israelianism of the work as a result of the Parisian inner art questions. Aharon Avni wrote, in the early 1940s: "Life is undergoing change under our very noses, and the only fundamental element in our lives is the Eretz-Israeli landscape. Hence, the landscape is almost the sole medium for original self-expression of Eretz-Israeli painting. The problems in landscape painting are therefore likely to determine the image of art in Eretz-Israel."

Menahem Shemi, subjected to trials and tribulations in his attempt to fuse personal experience with original style, from Picasso-like neoclassical static to pseudo-cubist expressionism, wrote: "Painting in Eretz-Israel (in the 1930s) is so detached from reality, from the landscape and whatever is transpiring therein, that it is as if it had never existed. The dark canvases in the exhibitions and the quest for subjects reminiscent of France indicate the artist's detachment from the reality and the nature in which he finds himself."

This same expressionism, in its Eretz-Israeli version, which became the hallmark of local painting from the 1930s to the end of the 1940s, close to the establishment of the State of Israel, is doubtlessly the result of the bond with Jewish Parisian Expressionism, that is, with the works of Kremegne, Mintchine, Aberdam, Max Band, Menkes, Dobrinsky, and, above all, the works of Chaim Soutine. These painters, like their colleagues in Eretz-Israel who came to Palestine in the 1920s, were born in Eastern Europe in the last decade of the Nineteenth Century. The period in which the first came to the East, out of Zionistic sentiment, they immigrated to Paris, and went on living as Eastern Jews, detached from their environment, hardly conversant in

YITZHAK FRENKEL, PLANTING, 1930's.

French. Their painting styles reflected stormy, restless souls. Exaggerated jesticulation, on one hand, and a penchant for lycricism, on the other, created their peculiar synthesis. Soutine's paintings comprise the exciting results of these spiritual and mental attributes, such as were inherent also in the contemporary Eretz-Israeli artists, in their native land and in the Eastern European environment in which they were raised. When the Eretz-Israeli artists reached Paris, beginning in the 1920s and in greater number in the 1930s, it was only natural that they should form ties with Eastern European Jewish

artists, some of whom had already become known in Montparnasse. In this circle were Modigliani, Chagall, Jacques Lipchitz and Kisling. They lived in "La Ruche" even before the First World War. The sculptor Hanna Orloff, working in their midst, had lived for some time in Little Tel-Aviv and participated in the Young Artists exhibition in the Ohel workers theatre. If we add to this the visualizing of the people from Palestine as national pioneers, of high status in the Jewish world, we shall come upon an almost natural bond between the painters who had come to Paris from Tel-Aviv, to be absorbed, taught and influenced by the artistic centre of the Western world, and the Jewish expressionists.

Yitzhak Frenkel, who as early as the 1920s inaugurated the connection between the Palestinian painters and the Jewish expressionist painters who migrated from Eastern Europe to Paris, also followed the course of abstractionism of Malevitch, until he developed an effective colourful painting in a stormy and dramatic manner. He gave an interesting testimony to the expressionist phase of Eretz-Israeli painting: "We sought, in art, strong emotions, and in Paris I strove to achieve a balance of the irrational elements within me. On the other hand, the paintings of the Jewish artists from Eastern Europe whom I met were characterized by compressiveness, dramatics, and distortion of forms . This character stems from coming up against French Romanticism. In Paris we were greatly influenced by the romantic expressionism of Delacroix. In the early 1920s, I was still under the impact of the days of hunger and terror of the October Revolution. I could not paint with a sense of balance and rationality. We were a minority marked by restlessness. Our baroque was an outcome of emotional exaggeration. We wanted direct and nonintermediary painting which transmits the emotional experience at the moment of its creation."

In the exhibits of the Massad and Egged groups held in Tel-Aviv in 1929, the influence of Parisian Expressionism was already clearly apparent in both the young artists of the Frenkel studio and relatively mature artists, like Gliksberg and Paldi. These exhibitions

ISRAEL PALDI, MOSLEM HOLIDAY, 1940-43.

JACOB STEINHARDT, THE GOLEM DREAM, 1935. WOODCUT.

actually brought to an end the period of David's Tower and the Hebrew Artists Association, and set off the phase of Eretz-Israeli Expressionism, which was to end with the shift to Abstractionism at the end of the 1940s.

At the end of the 1930s, Frenkel came to paint with a penchant for mysticism. The proximity to cabbalist interpretations and the atmosphere in Galilean Safad, where he worked, as well as his propinquity to Jewish subjects or contents, are given by him as the basis for these dark, red-blue paintings and for the introverted paintings with a filtered Rembrandt light.

At the same time the native Eretz-Israeli painter Moshe Castel returned from Paris. In Safad he created works whose mystical introverted atmosphere leans on the traditional Sephardic Jewish atmosphere, as crystalized in the life style of this community in Safad and Jerusalem. Castel arrived at this style after having searched for an original Eretz-Israeli expressionism in Persian miniatures and ancient Jewish manuscripts.

Mordechai Levanon's paintings of the late 1940s also reflect the mystification of the Galilean landscape and the city of Safad. This artist, Frenkel's pupil, addressed himself to the Eretz-Israeli landscape as to a pictorial idea, achieving a kind of range of hues dominated by a bluish tint, in an attempt to endow expression with a "cabbalistic exaltation."

Chaim Attar of Kibbutz Ein-Harod, the moving spirit behind the establishment of the museum at that kibbutz, returned from Paris in the 1930s, bringing with him extremist teachings of the Soutine style. Veteran artists, like Gliksberg and Shmuel Ovadyahnu, worked with no bond between them and the Jewish artists in Paris, in an expressionist style from which they had not freed themselves. Israel Paldi, who in the early 1920s had invested Arab fishermen with dynamic expression, returned from Paris in 1929 and began to create dark landscapes, prominently influenced by Expressionism: "In the dark painting I wanted to juxtapose my feelings and the Eretz-Israeli landscape. In order to give expression to the sharp, bright effulgence, which destroys the hue, my starting point was the dark background, for only from this darkness can we create a clear pictorial language." From 1936 until 1943 he reverted to themes of Eastern folklore known from the 1920s, this time emphasizing the pictorial elements: dividing the canvas into small areas,

SHIMSHON HOLZMANN, IN ACCO, 1937.
COLLECTION M. KADISHMAN.

40

LEOPOLD KRAKAUER, THORNS, 1935.
CHARCOAL DRAWING.

like tapestry. As opposed to the landscapes and Eastern life of the past with its accentuation of the exotic, he now had to contend with only pictorial problems, in the context of the same subject. He created works which while dealing with Moslem festivals, no longer idealized the image of the Arab but rather used the latter as the visible point of departure which was to lead him, still in the early 1940s, to his first collages, perhaps the first in Eretz-Israeli painting.

The 1930s also saw a relative settling down of art. The Tel-Aviv Museum was opened in 1932; that year also witnessed the first publication of "Gazit," the art and literature magazine. In 1933 a new phase began in local art: the expressionism of the artists, fleeing from Germany in the face of the Nazi ascendancy.

What distinguished the expressionist artists who came from Germany and Central Europe to Palestine beginning in 1933 was their perseverance in the style throughout their lifetime; most of them worked with this approach from their youth. In contrast, many Eretz-Israeli artists whose paintings were expressionistic in the 1930s veered off to other artistic concepts with a dynamism which indicated restlessness, searching and frequent change, parallel to the changes which the Jewish community in the country underwent in those days. The influence of Derain and Doufy on Nahum Gutman gave way to a graphic-expressionistic outburst in his reaction to the Arab rioting and massacre in Hebron, which signified the beginning of a new, harsh phase in the Arab antagonism toward Jewish settlement that was to grow

increasingly severe until 1936. This, along with the influx of Jews form Central Europe fleeing the Nazi domination, the rise of anti-semitism and the approaching Holocaust, engendered a sense of impending disaster. This may have been the cause, not felt in the beginning, of the shift on the part of Frenkel, Castel and Mordechai Levanon to the introverted mystic painting of the late 1930s and 1940s. It may well have accounted for the rising importance of Rouault, in his gloomy, religious paintings, and his influence on the Jewish artists in the 1930s. It could also have affected and explained the introversion and feeling of controlled sorrow in the paintings of Moshe Mokady, who was influenced by Rembrandt through the work of Max Band. For Aharon Avni and his colleagues, Corot and the Barbizon Group were a source of inspiration, but his works—for a time— became intimistic, in the wake of Vaillar. As his colours grew increasingly dark and the strokes of his brush more rapid and aggressive, according to the expressionist tradition, he was bothered by an extra-artistic question relevant to the problem oif identity: "I am taken up with the spiritual atmosphere of attachment to the soul of the homeland."

The extension of German Expresionism concentrated mainly in Jerusalem, in a German-speaking social nucleus around

MOSHE MOKADY, SEATED BOY, 1924.
OIL ON CANVAS. COLLECTION ISRAEL MUSEUM.

AHARON AVNI, ARAB·VILLAGE, 1940.
PEN DRAWING.

Anna Ticho and Leopold Krakauer, artists who had come to Palestine from Vienna in the 1920s (and had taken part in the exhibitions in David's Tower). In this social circle were several individuals from the Hebrew University, products of German culture: the philosophers Martin Buber and Shmuel Hugo Bergman, the scientist Leo Picard and the publisher Zalman Schoken.

In 1933, the most "Jewish" exponent of German Expressionism, Jacob Steinhardt, came to Palestine. Steinhardt was one of the founders of the expressionst Pathetiker Group in Berlin, together with Ludwig Meidner. He also displayed his works with the "Die Sturm" Group. His literary apocalyptic approach and sharp expressionistic style based on biblical themes did not change even when he was working on woodcuts in Jerusalem, on the schemes of Genesis and the Prophets. He populated his prints with Old City alleys and Eastern European religious experiences. The feeling of the burden of fate and the trauma of the Holocaust indirectly pervade his works, through biblical images and symbols.

The expressionist Yosef Budko, a disciple of Max Lieberman in Berlin, also arrived in Jerusalem in 1930. His subjects were the same as those of Steinhardt, who was a disciple of Lovis Corinth. These themes are associated with Jewish religious experience, for the most part; Budko's works are known here for their graphic creativity and their dramatic expression in black and white.

The German-speaking circle of artists and intellectuals in Jerusalem formed a kind of cultural aristocracy in a community whose leaders—in the arts, literature, economics and settlement—were mainly of Eastern European origin. What is important here is that the people of this immigrant influx governed the New Bezalel, the sole centre for arts and crafts studies, reopened in 1935 after its closure in 1929, despite the feeling that these Europeans were isolated; and that due to their failure to adapt themselves to the Hebrew language and the Eretz-Israeli mentality, their connections with the country's artists were greatly hampered.

Budko was named director of New Bazelel. After his death in 1940, he was succeeded by Mordechai Ardon, whose impact on the development of art in Israel was much stronger than that of his German-trained colleagues. In order to emphasize the influence of the artists of this move of immigration, it should be noted that Steinhardt directed New Bezalel as of 1953, when Ardon was appointed Artists Advisor to the Ministry of Education and Culture. Isidore Ascheim and Eisenscher also came from Germany to joined the New Bezalel staff.

The feeling of detachment between the German expressionists resident in Jerusalem and the Eretz-Israeli artists entrenched in Tel-Aviv was due also to reasons of artistic ideology: the local antagonism of most of the country's artists, whose painting was under the influence of French expressionism, against the German expressionistic painting. On the other hand, it was precisely in Tel-Aviv that the members of the German circle scored their most impressive gain: Dr. Karl Schwartz, who had organized, in Berlin, a movement of artists to Palestine, came there in 1933 and was appointed curator of the one-year-old Tel-Aviv Museum (founded in November 1932, at the height of the influence of Jewish-Parisian painting on the country's artists). Before the year 1933 ran its full course, an exhibition by *Artists Who Came From Germany* was mounted in the museum. Later there were one-man shows by Steinhardt, Budko, Ascheim and Krakauer.

Leopold Krakauer of Vienna came to Palestine in 1924, before the "German immigration." He was among the architects, born or educated in Austria and Germany, who wrote one of the most interesting chapters in Eretz-Israeli architectual history: Alex Baerwald designed the Haifa Technion in 1914; Richard Kaufmann among others, planned the cooperative settlement of Nahalal in the Valley of Jezreel, in 1920; Eric Mendelsohn set high architectural standards in planning some of the Hebrew University buildings on Mount Scopus, and the young architects, trained in the Bauhaus, among them Arie Sharon, Zeev Rechter, and Yossef Neufeld, made Tel-Aviv one of the more surprising examples of construction in the style and conception of the Bauhaus. Krakauer exerted tremendous influence on the formation of the kibbutz building style. His graphic works, mainly his drawings in black chalk, the themes of the mountains of Judah and the personification of olive stumps and brambles,

LEOPOLD KRAKAUER, JUDEAN HILLS, 1936.
CHARCOAL DRAWING.

became a trademark of the German school in Jerusalem. The emotional power emerging from his sketch sheets with "Van Gogh" dynamism, turned rocky slopes and vegetation in Jerusalem into symbols. Martin Buber wrote about him: "The event which marked his artistic fate was his encounter with the Jerusalem landscape. Krakauer's loneliness encountered the loneliness of the Jerusalem landscape, under the influence of which his loneliness turned into something different. It was only in his portrayal of the loneliness of the Jerusalem landscape that Krakauer became the kind of artist he was. The inner tension which determines the image, both vibrant and accomplished, of the thistle, the strong inner quivering which becomes frozen in the cutting of the limbs of the olive tree, like the sufferings of a human being, etched in the furrows of his face—all these emerge from Krakauer's paintings as the language of loneliness, the pangs of loneliness boring deep into the inner being of the painter."

Anna Ticho came to Jerusalem from Vienna in 1912. Sixty years later she was still held in great esteem as one of Israel's foremost drawing artists. In the beginning, in the 1920s and 1930s, she concentrated on detail-

JACOB STEINHARDT, CROSSING THE DEAD SEA. WOODCUT. COLLECTION ISRAEL MUSEUM, JERUSALEM.

ing scenes of landscapes and nature, in line with the Dürer tradition. She became attached, technically and emotionally, to the landscapes of the Jerusalem hills and the mountains of Judah, and her pencil sketched on the paper a kind of delicate filigree, creating a portrait of nature. Gradually she moved from treating the significance of the landscape to the qualities of the line which builds the landscape. Her subjects did not change, but as of the 1950s, her drawing lines are marked with expressive emotional drama; she no longer has need for drawing from nature, for in the course of abstraction she trasmits the pace and the essence of the landscape components. Elisheva Cohen, from the Israel Museum, wrote, in 1973: "Anna Ticho's last works are permeated with a soft yellow light of unrealistic beauty. But there is no trace of nostalgia here. This is the essence of the Jerusalem landscape, its difficult-to-explain nobility, its sadness and splendour."

The artists in the group which arrived from Germany in the 1930s came with technical know-how and skills. They were the ones who gave impetus here to the lithographic

JOSEPH BUDKO, A MAN LIKE ME WON'T FLEE, 1930. WOODCUT. COLLECTION ISRAEL MUSEUM, JERUSALEM.

arts, the woodcuts, etchings, and drawings, not only by means of their own creations but mainly in their courses of instruction at Bezalel. Isidore Ascheim studied in Breslaw with Otto Müller, a member of Die Brücke. Miron Sima studied in Dresden with Otto Dix, and Vienna-trained Jacob Eisenscher, developed in Eretz-Israel a synthesis of Expressionism and Cubism. A group of artists who were steeped in German and Viennese culture but whose style was not expressionistic, rounded out the artistic activity in this "European island" in Jerusalem. Ludwig Bloom painted colouristic-sentimental landscapes: Rudi Lehmann, the sculptor and influential educator (already a legendary figure), did work which bore affinity to the myths of the ancient East, and is therefore discussed in another chapter, relevant to this aspect of Eretz-Israeli art. To these we may add the poet and painter Elsa Lasker-Schuler; Hedwig Grossman-Lehmann, developer of pottery making, and other female

artists from Germany (who created a truly tangible feminine presence in the artistic community), as well as visits by such personalities as Alma Mahler. All these figures contributed to an additional phase in building the extraordinary model for implanting Western culture in the East. This was a result of the political upheavals which were beginning to shake Europe and Zionist ideology, which came to the consciousness of European Jewry in the wake of these upheavals.

The dominant figure in the group of German artists in Jerusalem, whose influence on the development and the molding of art in Israel was Mordechai Ardon; his activity ranged far beyond the relatively close confines of the group. Born in Poland, he absorbed the Eastern European Jewish religious tradition before coming to Germany as a student at the Bauhaus in Weimar.

In 1924 Ardon came under the tutelage of Klee, Kandinsky, Feininger and Itten, also serving as instructor in Itten's Kunstschule in

ANNA TICHO, JERUSALEM CITY WALL, 1930's.
PENCIL. COLLECTION ISRAEL MUSEUM, JERUSALEM.

ARIE SHARON, CONDOMINION FOR WORKERS, TEL-AVIV, 1933-35.

RICHARD KAUFMANN, NAHALAL, 1922.
VIEW FROM THE AIR.

Berlin from 1929 to his move to Palestine in 1933. Between learning and teaching he attended the Munich Academy, working with Max Doerner. The high technical skills he acquired from these two masters in the realm of colours, and the ideas garnered in the Bauhaus, made an indelible impression on Ardon. In his paintings he achieved an interesting synthesis between the Bauhaus innovations and Jewish apocolyptic content, religious sensitivities, and the symbolism inherent in the concepts of redemption and the return to Zion. Since 1953 his style has been conditioned by a strict technical processing of textures and colour values; Ardon is

JACOB EISENSCHER, JAFFA SCAPE, 1950's.

without doubt Klee's only pupil to combine Jewish symbols with the pure theories of painting which emerged from the Bauhaus. Ardon claims that the colours and forms in his paintings are "charms," the keys to a mystical world, and that his works give expression to the cabbala and hasidism. "Between the Tree of Life and the Tree of Knowledge there should have stood the Tree of Mystery, and the artist's place, between knowledge and life, is linked to the unknown." This may well be an echo of Paul Klee's words: "I wish to show the invisible."

Ardon's early, muted expressionism gave way to the creation of a metaphysical essence. The trauma of the calamity which befell European Jewry brought him back, without any apologies, to images belonging to the Jewish heritage, to scorched scrolls, to Jacob's ladder—and interchangeably, to burning landscapes of an Israeli desert and Eastern pagan twilights.

In Eretz-Israel Ardon sought the "key to the occult." He came out against new universal trends in local art. He viewed the New Bezalel as an arts-and-crafts school, similar to the Bauhaus, and it was he who gave the signal in Israeli art for the revival of metaphoric and figurative national painting, at the base of which lies the bond between Israel and the fate of the Jewish people. This concept, in his followers and disciples, direct and indirect, derives in most cases from the trauma of the Holocaust, clearly prominent in Israeli art as of the 1950s. The strict technical attention given to the traditional embellishment of the painting craft among these artists is also in accord with Ardon's preaching. Shmuel Bak, Yosl Bergner, Naftali Bezem, Shmuel Bonneh, and Avrahm Ofek are prominent figures in this trend. Another of Ardon's students, Yaacov Agam, who like his teacher also studied under Johanness Itten, took part in the founding of the kinetic and optical conception in Paris, in the early 1950s; but he also associated his works with concepts of the cabbala and Judaism, with Creation and the mystical, and Ardon's "key to the occult" apparently passed on to him.

With Ardon and his followers, the personal experience is also the national. The solution of the symbols is not Freudian, and the surrealistic figures derive from the trauma of the Holocaust or from the miraculous escape of the remnants and the move to Eretz-Israel. The routine religious symbols undergo change in the hands of these artists, most of whom regard their works as a mission on behalf of the destroyed Jewry, as indicators of historical events. For Naftali Bezem, who arrived in Palestine as a boy at the outbreak of Second World War (his family perished in the Holocaust), the boat symbolizes redemption, the return to Eretz-Israel. As he wrote: "I came here with the influx of migration, perhaps the most dramatic in the history of the human race. Together with my surviving friends, I flew across the heavens in a mighty sweep. Out of my body came a small winged

ALEXANDER BOGEN, JEWISH GIRL IN THE GHETTO, 1943. CHARCOAL.

With Shmuel Bak, a survivor of the horrible Wilno ghetto, a stringent technique attends literary painting. The clarity of the content is aided by a Renaissance style or one employed by the surrealists, but in an entirely different situation and far removed, spiritually. The unrealism of the subjects, the landscapes and the figures is the realism of Jewish history caught up in an incomprehensible holocaust.

Yosl Bergner brought to Eretz-Israel the household utensils and furnishings of a wiped-out family and community, and he implanted them in the swamps drained by the pioneers in Eretz-Israel. In his paintings, as in a book of Jewish legends, he gives the perished Jews a chance to reach the land of safe haven. The "realism of the imagination and the memories," pre-eminent in the early 1950s when Bergner came to Israel, at times gives way to expressionism, in order to depict falling angels—another sign of the deep sadness apparent in the figures of weeping women in the small Polish town whom his brush stations in the arched windows of Eastern houses in Palestine. His affinity to Magritte's style is one of pictorial technique rather than of content, where the existence of the painting

boat, which enfolded me like a protective shell. About me I saw the faces of parents, relatives and friends, hovering alive and above the abyss of murderous persecutions ... My plants blossom forth from ladders or boats." The motif of the ladder with Ardon, and the repetition of Jacob's Ladder also with Yaacov Agam, appear frequently in Bezem's works, as do the fish and the lion. But their significance is far from constituting a theme for painting. They relate to personal memories, tangent to the collective memories of a people: "My father would swing the fish above our heads, with one hand, as he murmured a prayer from a book in his other. The rooster pertaining to the expiating ceremony was this time disqualified, lest his crow should give us away, in those days of danger, and the fish substituted as the sacrifice. The fish is a mute creature, unable to cry out his protest." This exposition by Bezem, as well as his paintings and the ones by Bak and Bergner, are exactly identical with his works; this is to say, that the personal biography is also the biography of a people. Bezem is a concerned individual. He taught in Jewish refugee camps, and was one of the outstanding artists during the brief chapter of socialism in the early 1950s in Israel.

FRANZ KRAUSZ, ERETZ-ISRAEL
THE COUNTRY OF OUR FUTURE, 1934. POSTER.

**DAVID HENDLER, PORTRAIT OF THE PAINTER
LEVANON, 1934.** INK DRAWING.
COLLECTION ROSENFELD, TEL-AVIV.

RUDI LEHMANN, DONKEY, 1939.
WOOD.

**ZEEV BEN-ZVI, PORTRAIT OF THE ACTOR MESKIN,
1936.** BRONZE. COLLECTION ISRAEL MUSEUM.

49

RUDI LEHMANN, LADY WITH DOG, 1966.
WOODCUT.

YOSL BERGNER, FIGURES AND MASKS, 1955.

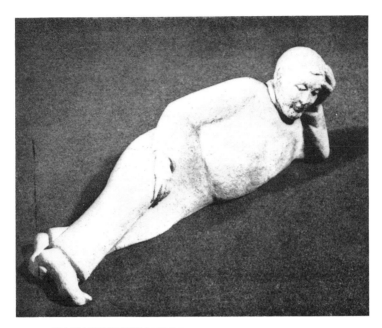

HEDWIG GROSSMAN-LEHMANN, RUDI LEHMANN WORKING, 1942.
TERRACOTTA.

AHARON GILADI, FIGURES, 1962. COLLECTION M. KADISHMAN.

lies in its extra-pictorial significance.

The paintings of Avrahm Ofek, who came from Bulgaria when Israel was established, chiefly depict the Jewish immigrant to Eretz-Israel. Permeke's approach to rough and direct sketching were in accord with Ofek's presentation of the immigrant as a displaced person, a peasant detached from his soil and planted in barren earth. Until the mid-1970s the saga of the anti-hero within the enthusiasm of the immigrant influx and the making of the land, the fate and loneliness of the individual, were the main aspects of his painting, which drew for style on Tamayo, Diego Rivera and the Florentine fresco painters. From this date on he abandoned painting and went into commentaries on the Bible, the Mishna and Gemara, seeking in the Jewish literary heritage the ideological and spiritual essence of the bonds with Eretz-Israel. The outcome of this ideology is found in the sculptured subjects relating to biblical and national myths and rituals.

Ardon and his followers represent the evolution which opposed abstractionism in Israeli art as of the beginning of the 1950s. The latter's protagonists were Zaritsky, Streichman, Stematzky and their colleagues, members of the New Horizons group, which influenced the local informal and the new currents in local art, from the mid-1960s to the present. This would indicate that the schism in Israeli art became clarified in the 1950s: aligning, on one hand, symbolic and textual art which strove for explicit national and Jewish expression; and, on the other, art inclined toward the abstract and the universal, which fostered the avant-garde currents of the following years.

The expressionist phase in Israeli art consists, as we have seen, of the influence of Jewish-Parisian painting from the mid-1920s, which gathered strength in the 1930s and continued into the 1940s, finally giving way to abstractionism. Expressionism of the German school was brought in, beginning in 1930, by refugee artists from Germany and Austria, with the rise of Nazism. Expressionist painting, in a different situation, was developed after the founding of Israel (beginning in the 1950s) by artists who personally underwent the horrors of war and the Holocaust in Europe; this terrible trauma became

the content of their creativity, an urgent testimony which had to be tendered.

As early as 1955 young Zvi Milshtein exhibited in the Tel-Aviv Museum images in a sharp and heavy expressionist style. Maryan came from the concentration camps and was in Israel in the late 1940s, before gaining a reputation in Paris. Broken in body and soul, Maryan regurgitated (in his expressionist paintings and their vigorous and aggressive strokes) the nightmares of torture, the defacement of the human image. He presented madness as the normal, the abominable and the desperate.

Osias Hofstatter came to Israel when he was already in his fifties. He was a refugee, preferring to work as a night watchman, as if he were still trying to escape the Gestapo horrors. For years he worked only in black inks on paper, making poor, unadorned works depicting fearful flagellated figures. He pressed into the paper as if trying to submerge the figures on its surface. His expressionist style grew out of the content, as the testimony

SHMUEL BAK, DAEDALUS AND SON, 1973.

52

YAACOV AGAM, MEA' SHEARIM, 1970.
STAINLESS STEEL. THE PRESIDENT HOUSE, JERUSALEM.

MARYAN, PAGE FROM THE AUTOBIOGRAPHY, 1975.

AVRAHM OFEK, IMMIGRANTS (DETAIL), 1972.
FRESCO.

OSIAS HOFSTATTER, MOVING, 1966.
INK.

of a victim fleeing from his nightmares. His pages are ascetic, black on white, and since his works derive from depression, it wouldn't be proper to find a parallel to them in the history of art of that period. Hofstatter's works are the result of historical events and not of the historical course of art.

The phenomenon of displaced persons, their arrival in Israel as an act of self-preservation or in the context of national ideology, and their attempt to create while torn between concepts of art and of a nation and their personal biography—these are characteristic of the complexity of art in Israel. The phenomenon of artists creating in the 1950s and 1960s, as well as at present, out of the trauma of the Holocaust and fears for their personal fate is detached from the devel-opment of present-day art, irrelevant to the language of art whose syntax does not recognize biographical labels or national stock-taking. However, it appears that expressionism is the natural tongue of fear, urgency, and depression. This holds true for Maryan, Hofstatter and also Thomas Kroner, who came from Vienna as a pioneer in 1938 and helped found a kibbutz; it was only after a silence which lasted more than twenty-five years that he went back to the personal and ascetic expressionist painting.

However, the expressionist conception is not limited here to a controversy between the French and German schools. It is also to be founded in the fundamental creativity of young artists functioning within the confines of the new art in Israel in the 1960s and 1970s.

AVRAHAM OFEK, LAMENTATION, 1961.
OIL ON CANVAS.

Chapter IV

The Redefinition
of Art in Israel

Around 1947 it became clear to a group of mature artists in Israel, that the struggle over the meaning and identity of art had reached a crucial point: for the painter Jossef Zaritsky and his circle, Streichman, Stematsky, Mairovich, Aroch, and a few other artists who formed the core of "Ofakim Hadashim" (New Horizons)—later the most influential group of painters in Israel—the move toward abstraction provided the only possibility of freeing Israeli art from national, provincial, Jewish expressionism and Oriental decorativism.

Their belief in this regard was part of an emerging cultural struggle concerning the identity of Israeli society, and not simply a question of artistic styles. After the Second World War and the Holocaust, the years which witnessed the struggle against the British mandate forces who ruled Palestine, the War of Independence with the Arabs, and the United Nations resolution on the right to found the State of Israel in part of Palestine in 1947 (which was accomplished the following year), were seen by these artists as constituting the most suitable historical moment for shifting Israeli art toward abstraction. Abstraction was identified with universality and with "normalization," with placing Israeli art on the same level as contemporary art in the West (one may recall the Zionist aim, at the beginning of the century, of "normalizing" the Jewish people by giving them a land of their own). The universality of the New Horizons artists was intended to free local painting from the Jewish expressionist influences which had dominated the art scene in Palestine since the end of the Twenties, and from the Jewish symbolism and scenery which had accumulated in local art beginning with the early Bezalel style of academicism

and quasi-Oriental decorativness, and had been compounded by the German expressionist artists who had immigrated to Palestine during the Thirties. All this blended reality with the Diaspora mentality. The antithesis was modern, nonfigurative, universal.

Zaritsky and his circle were not the only artists who strove in those days toward a redefinition of art in Israel. Beginning in 1939, a political and cultural circle gathered around the poet Yonathan Ratosh, who defined a clear theory of the identity and content of Israeli existence in Palestine.

The essence of this theory of the Young Hebrews, known popularly as the "Canaanites," is that the Jews, spread throughout the world, are not a nation but a religion. A nation means a community which lives in one territory, speaks one language, and shares political interests which derive from existence together in this territory. There is a gap of two thousand years in the history and culture of the Hebrew people, from their exile from Eretz-Israel, to their return in this century. This means that Jewish culture created in exile has no national affinity with the Hebrew people settled in Palestine, nor with their state. Israeli culture has to look back to its origins, to the Bible, intended here as a cultural rather than a religious document, and to find its roots in the civilizations of the ancient East situated between the Tigris and Euphrates valleys—the homeland of the Sumerians, Babylonians, Assyrians, and Hittites—and the Nile. This radical opposition to Zionism attracted only a few influential intellectuals and artists. It corresponded, in its demand to go back to ancient Eastern origins, to the concepts of the young sculptor Yitzhak Danziger, who executed the sculpture, *Nimrod*, in

Tel Aviv in 1939, soon to become a milestone in Israeli art. Danziger rendered this mythological hero-hunter, mentioned in the Bible, in reddish Nubian sandstone in an archaic style derived from ancient Egypt and Mesopotamia. His "Canaanitic" approach led him to the myths, rituals, and customs of Palestine; as well as to land art, in its broader stylistic and political meaning. His creations and concepts deeply influenced young Israeli artists from the late sixties onward, as will be seen below.

To return to Zaritsky and New Horizons, their activity led not only toward abstraction, but also toward other contemporary developments. The group made its first appearance in November 1948 in a show at the Tel-Aviv Museum. This fact marked a meaningful schism between national, local, Jewish, figurative art, and the new idiom, which was universal and abstract, after the artists' own definition. Zaritsky and his circle, were mature artists well reputed in Israel. Many of them—particularly those who later became the most influential, like Streichman, Stematsky, Mairovich and Aroch—had painted in the Jewish-Parisian-expressionist style during the Thirties and early Forties. Zaritsky, the undoubted leader, never experienced this approach, and his long stay in Paris at the end of the Twenties did not bring him under the influence of Soutine and Kikoine, an unusual fact in the biography of Palestinian artists who visited Paris during those years. Although he was a cultural star in the Twenties, he never shared in the Neoprimitivism that distinguishes this decade in modern painting in Palestine. His painterly solution to what he considered the most crucial problem in art from its beginning in Palestine—representing the local bright light—was to use transparent watercolours, leaving the white areas of the paper untouched. He remained attached to this technique, quite exclusively, for twenty-five years.

His intuitive interpretation of Cézanne's style led him to generalize the natural image, giving his watercolours a quasi abstract aesthetic. The long-standing pressure on artists in Palestine to reflect in their works the special character of the landscape and society, and to relate their creative vision to the "co-efforts of the nation," today cast some light on Zaritsky's characteristically unclear and rare definitions. In an interview in 1943, he said: "Art is the one and only God, and we must

YOSSEF ZARITSKY, COMPOSITION, c. 1947.
OIL ON CANVAS. COLLECTION ISRAEL MUSEUM, JERUSALEM.

YOSSEF ZARITSKY, ROOFS OF TEL-AVIV, 1940.
WATERCOLOR.

not worship Him partially." His approach to a "pure art language" was radical even for artists who participated in the New Horizons group, such as Moshe Castel who said, in the mid-Forties, "We have to free ourselves from strange influences and to strive toward originality. We shall find it by revealing the beauty of our landscapes, by feeling in our whole the burning desert and the ancient splendour of our mountains. As Jews we look in the arts for a new spirit and dynamic expression of sentiments and humanity."

Stematsky has to protect his art by writing, "Individual searches and freedom of the creative imagination do not oppose national art." The militant critic, Haim Gamzu, wrote in 1947, just before his nomination as director of the Tel-Aviv Museum: "Huge changes have passed on art in Israel in the last ten years, so that it is impossible now to use literary motives in painting; no one deals any more with biblical heroism; and art has freed itself from Oriental exotics."

The first event that awoke the public to the existence of an organized group around the concepts of Zaritsky, was the *Exhibition of the Seven* held at the Tel-Aviv Museum in

1947. The artists present included Zaritsky, Streichman, Stematsky, Mairovich, Aroch, Naton, Wexler and Giladi. But the chance to organize a larger show arose a year later, when an invitation to participate in the 29th Venice Biennale was sent directly to Zaritsky as head of the Israeli Association of Painters and Sculptors. He decided "undemocraticly", as he defined it, "to choose nine artists with a common art language" to participate for the first time, as Israelis, in the Biennale. Between the time the works were delivered and the opening, the proclamation of the State of Israel was made. Zaritsky was expelled from the Artists Association, and soon afterward New Horizons was founded around him.

New Horizons can be seen as a gathering of artists in a common search for modernism, as a change from all the styles which had developed in Palestine from the Bezalel aesthetic of the beginning of the century, up through Neoprimitivism and Expressionism. These artists formed a cultural and political circle, insofar as their artistic endeavours mirrored the politically meaningful process which took place at the same time and place.

Zaritsky's concept of the local within the

universal, by gradually passing toward abstraction, was interpreted in various and individual ways by New Horizons painters. One of the slogans that characterized their militancy was "against figurative painting." But, oddly enough, many of the founders of New Horizons, those who participated in the first exhibition in 1948, were heterogeneous in style, embracing figurativism and even realism.

Marcel Janco, one of the founders of Dada in Zurich in 1916, arrived in Palestine in

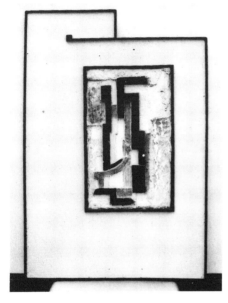

MARCEL JANCO, DADA RELIEF, 1918.
COLORED PLASTER. COLLECTION TEL-AVIV MUSEUM.

1941 as a refugee. His adoption by the founding members of New Horizons gave them the feeling of touching the European avant-garde. But Janco, from the mid-Forties in Israel, painted in an expressive Picasso-like manner far removed from his constructive-dadaist reliefs. He created and showed in the late Forties local socio-political subjects such a *The Wounded Soldier*, the black market, immigrants and their tents and camp-huts. Years later, he returned to an abstraction of organically shaped forms. Janco was the founder of the Ein Hod Artists Village, which still exists on the slopes of the Carmel Mountains, near Haifa.

Another example of representational painting associated with the early years of New Horizons may be found in the works of Yohanan Simon, then a radical-left kibbutz member who painted kibbutz life in accordance with a realistic aesthetic influenced by Diego Rivera's murals and by the earthy colours of Picasso's neoclassical works of the Twenties. Simon, a former disciple of Max Beckmann who attended the Bauhaus in the mid-Twenties, emigrated to Palestine in 1936. His adoption by the New Horizons circle was caused, partly, by his direct representation of the spirit of the kibbutz, appreciated then as an avant-garde society. During the Fifties he lived in Latin America, and the deep influence of the Brazilian vegetation on his style resulted in the decorative compositions which made his reputation.

The loose ideology of abstractionism espoused by New Horizons is also reflected in the Canaanitic representational sculptures of Kosso Elul and the Rouault-like human visions of Aharon Giladi.

The presence and impact of New Horizons as a pressure group and an organization which held yearly exhibitions of its members, lasted until 1963. Many of the artists who participated in the first exhibitions later left the group for ideological or personal reasons, and a sense of homogeneity characterized the last exhibitions. In the history of art in Israel, New Horizons is synonymous with abstraction. The term Lyric Abstraction, is applied the style of the hard core: Zaritsky, Streichman, Stematsky and, with some reservations, Aroch and Mairovich. But to what extent is their art abstract? The works of Zaritsky, Streichman, Stematsky and Mairovich were the result of direct impressions of the subject, mainly impressions of nature, its light and the characteristic colours of the landscape. The generalization of detail, in the passage from landscape, interiors, light and colours to the autonomous art language, creates a style which I prefer to define as Impressionistic Abstraction. These works are never imaginative and never planned a priori. Even if we find a quasi-geometric system in some of them, it is always a free interpretation of structures which were seen, or remembered, in nature or interiors.

These impressionistic abstract paintings are lyrical, in that they are introverted, inti-

AVRAHM NATON, FISHERMEN, 1951.

mate, done by a process of touching and covering, by transparent bright strokes and hints of hues. They are like a diary of sensibilities, accumulations of decisions and regressions. At their best, they are bright, dominated by white, grey, blue and pale pink, reflecting the problem of the representation of the local light central to painting in Israel since the beginning of the century. Over the decades it became important to judge the faithfulness of the work as Israeli art. Despite their demand to be universal, Zaritsky and his circle never abandoned their involvment in the representation of local light. Yehezkel Streichman said in a recent interview that his paintings are Israeli, because they express atmosphere and colour generated by the local light. In accordance with his multisemantic way of thinking, he adds: "Not light as a component of nature, but as a tool for expressing a unique spiritual situation, the situation of existence in this land in our time." He sees a suitable means for representing the Mediterranean light in the use of greys, and "not . . . yellows, as was thought by the old Bezalel teachers, as a result of their Eastern European fantasies about yellow deserts." Despite the rejection of Parisian Expressionism by the New Horizons artists, they inherited their grey light and lyric radiation from

the former.

The affinity between the sensibility and materiality of the works of Mark Rothko and Barnett Newman, and those of the works of Zaritsky and Ŝtreichman (done in the same years) led many observers to relate their qualities to the artist's common ethnic origin, and to the fact that all four painters were deeply conscious of their Eastern European Jewish cultural heritage. Zaritsky himself denies any correlation, affinity, or similarity with American painting, no doubt because his information about the abstract expressionist school was incomplete. On various occasions over the past fifty years he has declared that his art is French in its origin and aesthetics. He finished his art studies at the Academy of Kiev around the beginning of the First World War, and immigrated to Palestine in 1923. Thus he lived in Russia as a conscious artist in the historically tumultuous years of the Russian Avant-garde. But the only trace of Russian art from the beginning of the century that can be distinguished in his first watercolours done in Palestine, is that of Mikhail Vrubel (1856-1910), whose modern interpretation of Russian culture and pre-cubist style resulted in an acute sensibility toward colour and transparencies expressed in embryonic abstractions. And as Naum Gabo wrote: "Vrubel freed the

YEHEZKEL STREICHMAN, COMPOSITION, 1974.

AVIGDOR STEMATSKY, ABSTRACTION, 1970's.
COLLECTION ISRAEL MUSEUM, JERUSALEM.

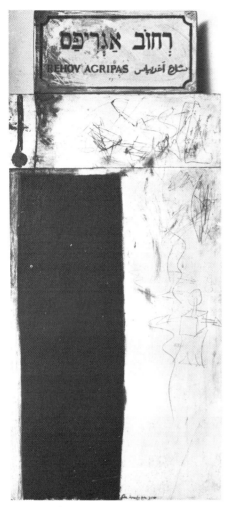

ARIE AROCH, AGRIPAS STREET, 1964.
ASSEMBLAGE.

art of painting from academic schemata." It is possible that the watercolours that Zaritsky executed during the Twenties were the result of the deep influence of this Russian artist, a protagonist of the avant-gardes, and that the works of Cézanne became a fresh source of inspiration only later, after Zaritsky's trip to Paris.

One must not underestimate the importance of Zaritsky's oil paintings from the late Forties in fixing Impressionistic Abstraction as the central trend in painting in Israel. In this context it is intersting to compare Vrubel's paintings from the year 1900 with Zaritsky's works from the mid-fifties on. In Vrubel's work *La princesse Cygne* (1900) one finds grey, blue, and pink brushstrokes creating passages and transparencies typical of Zaritsky's aesthetics fifty years later. Moreover, these hues, and particularly the pink, passed from Zaritsky to the abstract painters of the late Sixties, and characterized for some years the style of one of his most influential successors, Raffi Lavie. The influence of Bonnard and of Monet's later works on Zaritsky's abstract landscapes is likewise evident.

I emphasize landscape as an important subject matter for Zaritsky and his circle, because nature and its light substitute, for them, any obligation to deal with symbols and Eretz-Israeli clichés calling for an "Israeli art," a demand that, progressive as they were, they could not escape during the years of condensed national feeling, even in the socialist intellectual circle that supported the New Horizons concepts. The obsession with the representation of the local light can be exemplified in the works of Zvi Mairovich: in 1936, around the time of his arrival in Palestine, he painted a landscape in which the eye is concentrated on a white shining spot, representing the wall of a house submerged in vegetation. This white, the shocking sunlight, never disappeared from his paintings during the remaining forty years of his career. It can still be seen in expressionistic works, his abstractions, and above all in the pastel works done in the last eight years of his life (Mairovich died in 1974), which are among the outstanding achievements of Impressionist Abstraction. After his gradual shift to abstraction in the fifties, as one of the core members of New Horizons, he said, "I can't work without a starting point," and this point was always the immediate environment which surrounded him. "I am painting nature," wrote Mairovich, "and I have no intention of making this phrase more attractive." Indeed, he carried the New Horizon belief in the right to a free and individual interpretation of reality to its logical extreme.

Mairovich's close friend, Arie Aroch, shared the former's experiments with abstract pastel drawing in the mid-Sixties. But Aroch is connected more with the trends of Israeli art in the Sixties and even the Seventies, than with his generation, who strove from the late Forties for abstraction. Aroch, who arrived in Tel Aviv from Russia in his teens, passed the

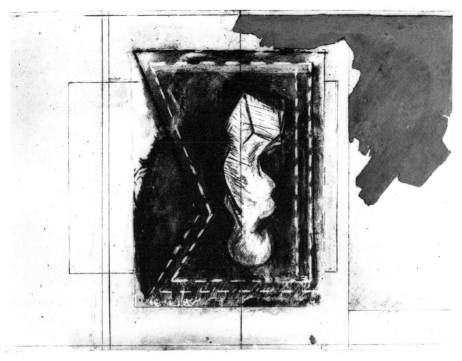

ARIE AROCH, FIGURE, 1970-71.

YEHIEL KRIZE, COMPOSITION, 1956.
OIL ON CANVAS.

phase of Parisian expressionist influence, which he remembers as his own Via Dolorosa: "The importance of the Ecole de Paris was its negative influence. For many years I could find no defense against the suffering and despair which this idea and phenomenon caused me from the very moment I came up against it personally in 1934. My feelings on the subject became stronger and turned into something like memories of a difficult childhood."   •

It is possible that this traumatic experience of a common and fashionable style led him to an approach which differed from lyrical abstraction. In the mid-Fifties his works were an exception to his environment. He used Dubuffet-like, innocent, childish images, including incised graffiti and scribbled lines. His nonobligation to style, subject, abstraction or figuration, unusual to his generation, and the substitution of all of this with the desire to do paintings as objects, made his works the most influential for the young generation of the Sixties. His works from that decade onward radiate the same kind of feelings as the objects of Joseph Cornell. In 1966 Aroch said: "I wanted to paint objects that were identifiable but also unconnected with the figurative and reality, like the forms which are found in abstract painting. I searched for a form that was definite, an 'object,' that is, the opposite of something chaotic."

He used found objects in his paintings, such as street signs and colour pages from magazines. Some of his best painting-objects include Hebrew letters and phrases, most of them with meaningful connections to his personal myths, which point back to the Jewish culture of Eastern Europe. He was an odd combination, an avant-garde artist (that is, an artist at the vanguard of the art scene in Israel) who "dared" to include Jewish emblems and meanings in his works. He describes a process of a "concrete" painting from the beginning of the sixties, thus: "I remember that in the city of my birth, Kharkov, a shoemarker's sign hung on a wall. There was a boot, and some gold remained on it. I remembered the sign as a 'work of art,' but when I tried to paint it from memory, I failed. I began to change the form with pencil, I deleted and added here and there until a form emerged that satisfied me as the form of a boot. When I looked at it

again, I knew that no one would believe that it was a boot. On the other hand, the form that developed from the boot was, in my eyes, concrete, as opposed to abstract. It had a right to exist, a right which I wanted to embody in the abstract object, as I defined it earlier." Aroch, in his intellectual, craftsmanly love of doing painting-like objects, was the only member of his generation related, in his works or concepts, to "classicists of the avant-garde" like Tatlin and Duchamp.

Moshe Castel and Aharon Kahana, two other New Horizons artists, advocated a stylized abstraction of biblical content. Castel, conscious of his Sefardic Eretz-Israeli origin, dealt in the late Twenties with Neoprimitivism based on Persian illuminated manuscripts. About ten years later, he represented a mystification of folklore in the Sefardic community in Palestine. His large canvases of streaming Hebrew words, in bright colourful compositions, shown at the beginning of the Fifties, yielded to scroll-like reliefs on canvas, done from ground basalt. Kahana, who immigrated to Palestine from Germany, contributed to the early New Horizons shows' imagery of biblical subjects schematized to reduced geometrical shapes. Moshe Mokady, remembered as an ascetic intimist in the Thirties, under the influence of the Jewish Parisian expressionists, shifted toward abstraction in the Fifties.

Outside of groups and gatherings, Yehiel Krize moved gradually toward abstract cityscapes, till he reached in the early Sixties white monochromatic compositions or multiplanar transparencies where white and grey dominate the surface of the canvas. His abstractions and the experimental works of Israel Paldi, who participated in the first exhibition of Hebrew artists in the David Tower in Old Jerusalem in 1921, were not included in the *New Horizons* exhibitions.

As early as 1943, Paldi began to create assemblages in mixed media. He used conglomerates, found pieces of wood, cement and papier-mâché for his informal relief paintings. In 1950 the first grotesque figures appeared, executed in sand, rope, plastic cement and oil paint. The affinity of this phase to the mixed-media figure paintings of Dubuffet, is clear. "The main source of my style is children's paintings," said Paldi. "In

64

ZVI MAIROVICH, JESUS IN A PRAYER SHAWL, 1961.

AHARON KAHANA, FIGURES IN MOON LIGHT, 1952.

their innocent and intimate approach to painting, children convert material into dream." He began in 1960 to create colourful paintings, using printed clothes, buttons, plastic jewellery, and sea shells.

The artists of Lyrical (or Impressionistic) Abstraction were not involved, as mentioned, in direct representation of the socio-political situation throughout the lifetime of New Horizons. Here, one is indeed surprised to find Yosef Zaritsky working in 1980 on a large abstract modification of Goya's famous painting, *The Execution*. This painting, done in Zaritsky's mature abstract style, is, no doubt, a result of anxiety and disappointment over the decline of Israeli society after the 1973 war.

Yeheskel Streichman, the "most lyrical painter of Lyrical Abstraction," showed in his retrospective at the Tel-Aviv Museum in 1975, a large painting executed in that same year which is unusual in his opus: within the rich, colourful structures, a woman, like a white shining sculpture, stands near the distorted grid of the window. Through the broken glass, heavy dark vegetation penetrates into the room, the artist's studio: the mother mourning over her dead sons, is surrounded by a war atmosphere of tension and fear. This unusual subject and image, like that

of Zaritsky, done in the traumatic years which followed the '73 war, is an "Israeli Guernica." Streichman says, "We made a mistake in that our paintings did not express the anxiety and tension of our life in this land. How could an artist in this place, so saturated with the struggle of existence, be detached from his environment? It's unbearable today to paint and to say 'my painting is like a bird singing on a tree.' No, we have to express real life; I confess I did not do so in the past." One has to remember that those two works by the mature and influential masters belong to a time when contemporary art in Israel was deeply involved with political subject matter.

The strategy of the art of the Fifties was concentrated around New Horizons and its antagonism toward national symbolism and Jewish Expressionism, both of which were associated with Mordechai Ardon, who dominated Jerusalem as the New Bezalel Academy director and later as the art advisor to the Ministry of Education and Culture. Two of his best known disciples, Avigdor Arikha and Yaacov Agam, so radically different in their intellectual concepts and artistic styles, moved to Paris at the beginning of the decade. Others, like Avrahm Ofek and Naftali Bezem, took part in the Israeli version of social realism.

65

In Tel-Aviv, several students of the Streichman-Stematsky studio, the nonestablished incubator for modern painting created in 1945 in an underground space, came back from the War of Independence to organize themselves as an artists group under the name of "The Ten." One of the ten, Eliahu Gat, said, on this subject: "As a sociable impulse and to prove to our teachers that we exist as artists we decided to create the group. Our first exhibition took place in 1950. We did not rebel, we looked for the encouragement of the mature New Horizons artists. We did not have information about current art trends in the West, as the New Horizons did not have, because the Second World War cut all the ties with the outside, and we understood that direct representation of nature would lead us to an original Israeli expression. This opposed New Horizons concepts, and we were pushed toward radicality, as can be seen in the manifests of The Ten, which called for a tightening of the bonds between artists and the landscape, its characteristic light and colours, to express our roots as a nation that lives on this earth." It is interesting how such an approach reminds us of the Aklim group in the mid-Seventies, of which Eliahu Gat is also a central figure. Conversely, it is similar to the demand of Eretz-Israeli artists of the Twenties. The Ten existed as a group with annual shows till 1960. Among its members one finds Zvi Tadmor, Clair Yaniv, Ori Raizman and Moshe Prupes with Efraim Lifschits, who participated in the late exhibitions of New Horizons; other students of the Streichman-Stematsky studio, the second generation of Israeli abstraction, like Lea Nikel, Michael Argov, and David Lan-Bar, spent the Fifties in Paris, where they tightened their bonds with European abstract trends. In the Fifties, Paris again become a place of pilgrimage for Israeli artists, after a decade of isolation caused by World War II and the War of Independence. The Israeli artists in Paris included a cross-section of generations, who were thirsty for new information and inspiration, but no longer through the Jewish school of Paris, which lost its vitality and magnetism at the end of the Thirties. The veteran Israeli, Paldi, created there his monochromatic abstract reliefs, after revealing an astonshing affinity between his assemblages, done earlier in Palestine, and the *brut* works of Dubuffet. Among New Horizons artists, Kahana and Castel frequently visited Paris, and Yosef Zaritsky journeyed to the city on his first trip outside Palestine in twenty-five years possibly as a result of the visit to Tel-Aviv of Willem Sandberg, from the Stedelijk Museum in Amsterdam. Sandberg acquired some paintings by Zaritsky for his museum, where Zaritsky held a one-man show in 1955, after his stay in Paris. Lea Nikel executed in Paris, as early as 1954, completely abstract collages with feathers, gold leaves, rags and newspapers on a colourful, effective, oil-painted support. Exhibiting in the Parisian gallery of the Cobra group, she fell under the influence of Wols and Bissière. When she returned to Israel in 1961, her dynamic "fauve" colourfield paintings seemed nearer to the New York School and more radical than the dominant Impressionist Abstraction.

The newly emerged Nouveau Réalisme became influential to young artists of the early Sixties, such as Yehuda Neiman, Igael Tumarkin, and Aika Brown (who also felt the impact of Tàpies).

An interesting group of sculptors, in the Israeli artist colony in Paris, was detached from the currents of the art metropolis: Achiam, Shlomo Selinger and Amos Kenan continued to work along the lines of Canaanite ideology. Avigdor Arikha and Yaacov Agam arrived in Paris at the beginning of the Fifties where they still live and work. Although their mentalities and concepts of art differ, they share a strong identity as Israeli artists. Arikha arrived in Palestine in 1944, from Eastern Europe, as a refugee child. At the beginning of the Fifties he gained a reputation in Israel for his subtle, linear drawings and illustrations, notably for books by Rilke and Hemingway (Arikha also executed drawings during the Seventies, for works by his friend Samuel Beckett, who wrote an essay on Arikha's drawings). Beginning in 1957, Arikha moved to abstract painting based on a language of broken rectangular planes, expressing deep emotionality with light and shadow. Away from the Israeli abstract mainstream, he speculated on the meaning of painting, and published essays of

AVIGDOR ARIKHA, SELF-PORTRAIT SHOUTING ONE MORNING, 1969. INK.

art theory. He spoke about the artist being trapped between a growing clarity of conscience and a diminishing experience of belief. In 1965 he stopped painting and passed to an eight year period of drawing "from nature." In this connection Robert Hughes writes, "Arikha has produced some of the most remarkable images on paper since the death of Giacometti. Arikha draws in order to see, as a writer might write in order to think. There is probably not an artist of his generation who has shown so vividly the questions and feedbacks that beset the strange activity known as drawing from life." In 1973 he passed from ink-drawings to oil paintings, mainly of indoor images in their natural size. "I freed myself from Cézanne and from the fear of local colour," he says.

Until the Fifties Marcel Janco was the only Israeli artist who took part in the creation of an international art movement (Dada, in 1916). The young Yaacov Agam arrived in Paris in 1951, from his birthplace on the dunes south of Tel-Aviv, to become one of the pioneers of kinetic art. He took part in the historical exhibition *Le Mouvement* (with Tinguely, Soto, and Vasarely) at the Denise René Gallery in Paris, in 1954, after showing his first polyphonic paintings. Agam's art is based on the concept that reality is ever-changing; that nature and human existence are in an eternal process of formation. His

theory, gaining a broader reputation abroad than in his homeland, combines Jewish philosophy with his kinetic-up-to-date technology of electronics and computers. "Reality is unseen. Reality is imaginary. After the concepts of Judaism, everything is eternally in process; it survives, but does not exist. These concepts oppose Pharaonic culture, which strives to eternalize, to mummify, to stop the flow of time." He correlates the techniques of revelation in cabbalistic Jewish mysticism with that of artistic creation. In 1973 he showed in the Tel-Aviv Museum his computerized "water and fire" sculpture, minimal kinetic works, and multifaceted paintings.

The decade that followed the end of the War of Independence and the creation of the State of Israel in 1948 was characterized by a turmoil of crucial problems: security and economic crisis and mass immigration from Europe, from Islamic countries in the Orient and North Africa, which caused a sharp change in the demographic and cultural image of close, familiar Israeli society. Social ideals seemed to crumble under the enormous weight of Zionism and statehood. Prior to 1948 this society had passed a decade of deep anxiety caused by the Second World War and the Holocaust, which murdered its families and erased its cultural past in Europe; fol-

SHLOMO VITKIN, COMPOSITION, c. 1963. OIL ON CANVAS.

lowed by an intensive guerrilla war against the British mandate forces in Palestine for the purpose of establishing independence and creating a homeland for Jewish refugees (the Jewish population of Israel doubled during the three years which followed the founding of the state, reaching about a million and a half persons in 1951); and then by the bitter War of Independence. Against this background, two socio-cultural considerations can help one understand the episode of Social Realism which was played out in Israel in the decade following 1948. One consideration is the struggle for an effective socialist state. The ruling establishment of the actual state, and before it the state-in-the-making, was socialistic and included the labour parties. Nevertheless, it seemed to the radical Zionist-socialist movement, and mainly to the idealistic society of the kibbutzim (which was part of this movement), that the leadership of Ben Gurion, the prime minister, and his moderate socialist party and governmental coalition, tended to ignore authentic socialist ideals, striking compromises with the clerical parties and with the subscribers to economic support in capitalist centres. They reacted bitterly toward security policy (particularly the limitation of the right of the Arabs who remained in the villages and towns included in the Israeli territories after the 1948 war), and they interpreted the high unemployment rate among immigrants and the difficult conditions in the camps of tents and huts as oppression of the masses. The style and language of these groups' demonstrations were borrowed from the Russian communist regime; for, until 1953, the education and the cultural goals of socialist youth in Israel were those of Russian communism. Paradoxically, this socialist environment and education, deeply Zionistic, excluded the non-Zionist Communist Party and individuals, and fought against them more bitterly than against the right-wing nationalist and clerical parties and organizations. Behind the demand, voiced by the radical-left Zionist parties and kibbutz intellectuals, for a "culture for the masses," opposed to "art for art's sake," and based on the concepts of Stalinist Zhdanovism and the radical-Marxist art theories of Lukacs (translated and well known in Israel at the time), stood a struggle over the content that Israeli society would take in its independent homeland. At the same time, New Horizons artists were struggling for abstraction and international modernism. The second consideration regards the artistic and political propensity toward figuration and realism in opposition to abstraction; or in other words, toward direct expression of the socio-political struggle of the proletariat, as a visual translation of universal slogans (such as peace, justice, bread and work, equality, and unification of the proletariat) translated into local terms.

Most of the social-realist artists came from the circles of the Hashomer Hatzayir youth movement and its kibbutzim, both of which belonged to the Mapam leftist labour party. We call Social Realism an *episode* in Israeli art history, because its adherents' art products were secondary to their political activity, illustrations and demonstration-signs prevailing over the concept of paintings. For example, Dani Karavan, who was an active member of this circle, never executed an artwork defined as social-realist. Avraham Ofek and Dan Kedar seldom did so, and even the radical Shimon Zabar was considered one of the most gifted landscape artists before he left Israel for political opposition activity in London in the Sixties. Moshe Gat grew up in a slum in Haifa, and his woodcuts of workers in iron factories, and of shoemakers and tailors in small workshops, all done in the spirit

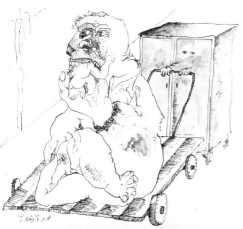

URI LIFSHITZ, DRAWING, 1970.
COURTESY GORDON GALLERY, TEL-AVIV.

MOSHE GAT, SEAMSTRESSES, 1955.
OIL ON CANVAS.

YOHANAN SIMON, WORKERS, 1947.
OIL ON CANVAS.

of Frans Masereel, indicate the atmosphere within which this group of artists worked. The now-forgotten Avraham Braunstein, then an immigrant living in the tumble-down quarter deserted by the Arabs in Jaffa, shocked his public with a large painting showing children playing with a dead mouse, as their only toy, in a slum. Naftali Bezem reacted to an event which brought scandal to Israeli society in 1953, when a strike of sailors in the port of Haifa was put down with agressive force by the socialist government. His large panel painting, *For Solidarity with the Sailors*, shown in the same year in the general exhibition of Israeli artists, includes the unemployed and tents in an immigrant camp. The spirit of Guttuso and Realismo, admired by Bezem during his trip to Italy; the impact of the Mexicans Diego Rivera, Orosko and David Siqueiros on the paintings and murals of the militant Gershon Knispel; and the reproductions of Käthe Kollwitz hung in kibbutzim dining rooms, as well as the works of Ruth Schloss, all clarify the atmosphere of the social-realist circle. Yohanan Simon, then a kibbutz member, painted in the early Fifties images of kibbutz folklore in earthy colours and broad volumes which recall Picasso's return to classicism in 1921-23 as well as the murals of Rivera for Rockefeller Center, seen

by Simon in New York in 1935. Yohanan Simon was a well reputed artist within the intellectual circle of the Hashomer Hatzayir leftist kibbutz movement, and so, a part of the social-realist front; but surprisingly enough, he was also a founding member of the New Horizons group, which opposed literary or direct figurative representation. Marcel Janco, the Dadaist, was involved in the early Fifties in representing stylized social-realist subjects. These artist's detachment from New Horizons can be seen as a result of their desertion from the abstract camp toward local representational subjects.

Whereas Paris had a magnetic effect on Israeli artists who shifted toward abstraction in the Fifties, the pole of attraction for the social-realist artists was Italy for studying wall-painting techniques and for executing actual works in public spaces (Karavan, Ofek, Bezem), as well as Mexico for its school of monumental painting (Moshe Gat, Knispel, Yohanan Simon). The disappearance of the social-realist tendency toward the end of the Fifties was due not only to the overall success of the dominant New Horizons group (who succeeded in establishing an art language while the young realists vacillated between political activity and immature expression), but also and mainly to the sharp decline in the

69

AVIVA URI, SEATED FIGURE, 1958.
BLACK CHALK. COLLECTION I. ZAFRIR, TEL-AVIV.

in new and abstract directions. In 1958, the Bezalel Museum (later included in the Israel Museum, opened in 1965) showed an exhibition entitled *Twelve Artists,* curated by the young Yona Fisher. Mixed in its concepts, this show gives one an idea of the new art scene of those days. Together with the Tamayo-and Permeque-like heavy, earthy, figurative scenery of Avraham Ofek, the surrealistic vision of Yossl Bergner, and the symbolic paintings of Shmuel Boneh, one finds the fruits of the struggle of New Horizons to create an atmosphere of Modernism: Aviva Uri, disciple of the veteran drawing master David Hendler, exposed works in pencil and chalk which reduced lines in nature to free, autonomous handwriting. These works, shown a year earlier in the Tel-Aviv Museum, had a decisive impact on the young painters of the mid-Sixties. Abstract paintings by Lea Nikel and the bright watercolours of Louise Schatz, along the lines of Klee, together with Michael Gross's first radical reductions of landscapes provided a promise for the future.

belief of the Zionist left in Stalinism as a result of radical actions against Jews and Zionists in the popular democracies (such as the trial against Jewish doctors in Russia in the mid-Fifties). It is possible that the anonymous painters in the Communist Party clubs, immigrants from Eastern Europe who maintained no contact with the art circles, were the real unknown heroes of social realism in its Israeli version.

At the beginning of the Sixties, the dominance of New Horizons inhibited the acceptance of relatively young artists who worked

The rise of the new generation of artists was not accompanied by the usual rebellion of sons against fathers. The latter, the leading figures of New Horizons abstraction, began in the late Forties to pave the way for the new possibilities of painting, incorporated young artists (Lifschitz, Kupferman, and Azen,

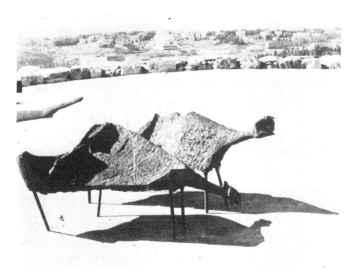

ITZHAK DANZIGER, SHEEP, 1954.
BRONZE. COLLECTION ISRAEL MUSEUM, JERUSALEM.

among others) in their last exhibition in 1963 at the Ein Harold Kibbutz Museum, and participated together with their younger counterparts in group exhibitions like *Tazpit,* in 1964, at the Tel-Aviv Museum. The protagonists of the Sixties and the Seventies, the second and third generation of abstract painters, appeared in solo or group shows during the period from 1958 to 1965. The latter year witnessed the creation of "10+," the strategic organ for exhibitions which mirrored the arrival of new concepts on the Tel-Aviv art scene. Different in spirit from Israeli abstraction, 10+ marks the transition from that phenomenon to the new trends of the Seventies. In addition, 1965 is the year in which the Israel Museum, which became a supporter of new trends on the local art scene, was created.

The impact of the early works of Aviva Uri, shown in the Tel-Aviv Museum in 1957, on young artists of the sixties, resides not so much in her abstraction, as in her definition of line as a language. She isolated the line on the whiteness of the paper to expose the sensibility of the hand and the eye, using it as a seismograph of the inner self. It looked *povera,* humble, when compared to the rich and festive colours and planes of Zaritsky, Streichman or Stematsky's Lyrical Abstraction. She dematerialized the painting, freeing it also from its ceremonial process. To Raffi Lavie and his generation she provided an outlet from the virtuosity and saturation of the masters of Impressionistic Abstraction. In its simplicity and spontaneity, the new drawing looked suddenly and naturally Israeli. The works of Aviva Uri from the late Fifties onward were the seeds which sprouted the shift toward "epistemic" drawing, in the 1970s.

From 1960 oward, a similar presence dominates the paintings of Moshe Kupferman, who arrived in Israel as a survivor of the Holocaust in 1948 to become a founding member of a kibbutz named The Ghetto Fighters. His works from the late Sixties look like an abstract-expressionist distortion of Agnes Martin grids. His first exhibited paintings radicalized Zaritsky's style toward an expressionist explosion. The grid, as an obsessive component in almost all his works up to the present, is painted, erased, covered or incised into the material of the paint. Kupferman intensifies the process of making a painting, with quick black and white brush-drawing set in deliberately ineffective, grey-violet, muddy colours. The illusion of a transparent, deep multiplicity of planes is caused by the process of covering which hides more than it reveals. Any constructed plane is immediately destroyed or erased. This process of decisions and regressions makes Kupferman a successor of Zaritsky and Streichman. In case, however, no starting point in nature can be found.

In 1961 Igael Tumarkin returned to Israel after a five-year stay in Europe. A painter, sculptor and stage designer, Tumarkin played

IGAEL TUMARKIN, THE PORTRAIT OF THE ARTIST AS A YOUNG FIGHTER, 1966.
BRONZE. COURTESY GORDON GALLERY, TEL-AVIV.

the role of the protesting artist, ever in the news, using mass communication with endless energy to react against political events and art politics. Adopted by the art establishment, he executed about forty monuments and projects in the open, accompanied by relatively rare personal exhibitions in the Jerusalem and Tel-Aviv Museums. Born in Germany in 1933, and brought up in Israel, he worked in the mid-Fifties, for about two years, as assistant stage-designer with the Ber-

DOV FEIGIN, CONSTRUCTION, 1958.
IRON.

MOSHE SHTERNSHUSS, SCULPTURE IN MITSPE
RAMON, NEGEV, 1962.

thold Brecht Theater in East Berlin. The bit-
ing political art of George Grosz, Raoul
Haussmann and John Heartfield in Germany
between the two world wars comprise the
basic source of his approach. His "combined
paintings" of the early Sixties, the sharp cut of
the canvas, the dark paint with red drippings,
bear the direct influence of Tàpies. During the
Sixties he created aggressively expressionistic
cast-bronze sculptures of his face and body,
combined with machine-gun relics. These
traumatic anti-war impressions foreshadow
the war of October 1967.

Tumarkin's interest in collage and the
combination of different materials led him to
use minimal stainless steel and rusted iron in
the same work, or brightly coloured paint on
found junk. In 1978 he wrote: "My creation is
a collection of accessories and traces from the
environment, that have lost their functional
capacity in the process of creation, and are left
as clues, if you wish, symbols of civilization."
An interest in using sunlight and solar energy
is reflected in a concrete and steel construction in the open, built in 1968 on the hill of
Arad overlooking the Judean desert.

Characteristic of Tumarkin's activity over
the years, is the inclusion in his works of
information about other artists' works, such
as the inscriptions of protest or homage in
most of his drawings. In his own words, "I
make subjective journalism. The environment, current events, pass through a filter
named Tumarkin. The result is my creation."
One of the largest public works which he
planned, the Monument to the Holocaust
and Revival, erected in the municipal square
of Tel-Aviv in 1975 in cortex and glass, combine in a minimal style, bold symbolism of the
Star of David, the Yellow Patch, and drip-
ping waters as tears of mourning.

The memorial monuments which can be
seen throughout Israel are the result of a history of struggle and tragedies in Palestine and
abroad. The first sculpture in the open, built
in the mid-Twenties, the famous *Lion of Tel-
Hai,* is a memorial to those who fell in the
battle for the right of a commune of pioneers
to settle on the land. Hana Orloff's sculpture
in bronze representing a young lion (of Judea)
struggling with the Lion of Albion, near Tel-
Aviv, is a memorial to the victims of the
struggle for independence against the British
mandate forces, between the end of the

Second World War and the War of Independence. The only woman sculptor among the Tower of David artists, Batya Lishansky, built the large-scale stone figurative memorial in Kibbutz Hulda.

A growing interest in sculpture resulted in 1962 in the Mizpe Ramon symposium for sculptors, which took place on the edge of a crater in the Israeli dessert (Negev). It included some examples of abstract stone sculpture by the veteran New Horizons artists, Dov Feigin and Moshe Shternshuss, and it provided a correlation between abstraction in painting and abstraction in stone. The same correlation can be found in the welded iron abstract sculptures, bearing associations with organic forms, done by Yitzhak Danziger, from the mid-Fifties; and by Yehiel Shemi, a young participant in the *New Horizons* exhibitions. Shemi, a kibbutz member, became from that time on a major creator of metal constructions (environmental sculptures and works in nature) and memorial monuments.

The *Negev Monument* by Dani Karavan (1963-68) is a "sculpture village," intended to commemorate the struggle to safeguard the water pipeline to the new settlement in arid

YEHIEL SHEMI
MEDITERRANEAN SUN, 1964. IRON.

YEHIEL SHEMI , SCULPTURE, 1981.
IRON.

73

southern Israel during the War of Independence. Karavan used here elements from nature as building materials for an environment: a water line (a lifeline, in his description), sunlight, the blowing wind. Along the monument's axis, a channel of streaming water is directed toward a dome cut in the centre to allow sun to create a line of light in the dark interior. A serpentine bunker tunnel is cut into rectangular segments so that the sunlight penetrates the apertures so formed and creates a sequence of linear light frames. The use of lines of light and water as drawings in nature became central to Karavan's works in the 1976 Venice Biennale, in Documenta in 1977, and in his environments at the Forte Belvedere in Florence in 1978, as well as in his design for the axial environment in the new city, Cergy-Pontoise, near Paris, in 1980. From the group of orchestrated geometrical and organic volumes of the Negev monument rises a cylindrical structure, twenty metres high, resembling a flute perforated with apertures (and including a system of metal wind-flutes) through which the passage of the wind makes music composed by nature. In this context, Bruno Zevi defined Karavan's work as "an array of intimate internal spaces in which a mysterious totemic dialogue is created."

The entire monument is built in accordance with a system of "intuitive measurement," a characteristic approach later emphasized by Karavan in his "environment for peace" in the Venice Biennale, which drew the visitor into a space of pure metaphysical feelings.

The "visual acoustics" devised by Le Corbusier in planning the Ronchamp church in the early Fifties can be related to Karavan's creative climate. On the concrete walls, lines of letters flow together to create a microenvironment of information recording the events which this monument commemorates. The flow of lettering, imbedded in the concrete, with footsteps and scribbling, recalls the low reliefs and stone tablet epistles of ancient Hebrew, Egyptian, and Sumerian cultures. The same low relief concept is demonstrated by Karavan in his large stone wall in the Assembly Hall of the Israeli Parliament in Jerusalem, executed in 1966.

The water lines in the *Negev Monument*, as in later projects by Karavan, are fed from old irrigation canals in sharon groves and from the ancient line of water which threads its way in the Judean desert toward Jericho. The foot-and handprints on the surface of the concrete, are closely related to Karavan's personal myths. Born in 1930 in Tel-Aviv, then a

DANI KARAVAN, THE NEGEV MONUMENT, 1963-68.

MENASHE KADISHMAN, WAVE, 1969.
STAINLESS STEEL AND GLASS. COURTESY HIRSHORN MUSEUM, WASHINGTON.

small city set amid the sand dunes of the Mediterranean shore, he remembers, "With my bare feet, as a child, I first felt forms impressed into the sand. My footsteps in the sand were my first relief; the sunlight discovered them. The dunes were the first environmental sculpture, ever changing, on which my shadow told the time." Personal and cultural myths of Palestine and the ancient East are also central to the activity of one of Israel's most influential figures, Danziger, and much emphasized in the works of Menashe Kadishman, mainly from the Seventies. The art establishment in the mid-Sixties was not prepared for such concepts as Karavan's; Haim Gamzu, for instance, was still dealing with the fact that "The School of Paris overcame German Expressionism and even gained a victory over the Slavic influences in our painting." And the Israel Museum showed consistency by not showing any work by Karavan, until quite recently.

Toward the mid-Sixties the change of guard between the generations reached completion. The young and energetic painters who "were born into the abstract," the "state generation" who started their creation after the establishment of Israel as a state, looked for a social and organizational outlet from the New Horizons circle of their teachers. As was mentioned above, the first annual Tazpit exhibition took place in 1964, a year after the last New Horizons exhibition, accompanied by a declaration stating, "We oppose any plastic expression based on expressionism, and refuse any connection with 'Jewish iconography,' as well as any other abuse of symbolism which has lost its meaning long ago, and which, to our regret, still finds a response among idle circles of the public and its institutions," and specifying, "We do not strive for any sensational discoveries or for any revolu-

MENASHE KADISHMAN, SUSPENSE, 1966.
PAINTED IRON.
COLLECTION ISRAEL MUSEUM, JERUSALEM.

tion in art." This promise of competence was directed toward the still-powerful leaders of New Horizons, whereas the first phrase reveals a conflict with the director of the Tel-Aviv Museum (which hosted this same exhibition), whose suspicion of innovation placed him at odds with young artists till his retirement in 1977. Gamzu, a strong personality who began building the new Tel-Aviv Museum in 1971, fulfilled the imposible mission of "art dictator" in the crowded and overenergetic art circle of Tel-Aviv.

Gallery, the first and only gallery to work intensively with the new generation. It changed the art circle's concept of a gallery. In the atmosphere of renovation which gave rise to the Gordon Street galleries, the director S. Yariv showed, acquired and even sold the works of Raffi Lavie, Uri Lifschitz, Tumarkin, Kupferman, Aviva Uri, and later, of the young Druks and Garbuz. Although the art-world style of Tel-Aviv continued to prevail,

MOSHE KUPFERMAN, FROM "POPULATED WORKS", 1979.
CRAYONS ON PAPER. COURTESY GALLERY GIMEL, JERUSALEM.

The most meaningful formation of young artists was 10+, who appeared in their first show in 1965. They inherited from their New Horizon fathers (Zaritsky was also a co-director of the Hebrew Artists Organization in the Twenties and the head of the Israeli Association of Painters and Sculptors till 1948) the tradition of organizing in groups in order to exhibit. Our definition of the New Horizons organization can be equally applied to 10+: they were not homogeneous in style, and a curiosity toward modernism was a criterion of their activity. The appearance of 10+ paralleled the opening of the Gordon

the opening of the Israel Museum in 1965 provided a patron-museum for new artistic expressions.

The 10+ group was initiated mainly by Raffi Lavie and a core of friends including Yoav Barel, Aika Brown, Ziona Shimshi, Buky Schwartz and Efrat, among others. Their typically Israeli "Sabra" approach called for a veneer of art-as-a-game, of naughtiness, over greater ambitions and deeper concerns.

Raffi Lavie (born 1937 in Tel-Aviv), has contributed to Israeli art as a painter and teacher, advocating the demystification of painting and a less acute differentiation between everyday activities and "creation."

AVIVA URI, LANDSCAPE, 1971.
BLACK CHALK. COLLECTION M. SPITZER, JERUSALEM.

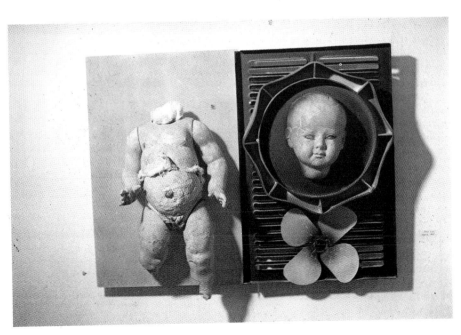

YOAV BAREL, OBJECT IN RED, 1966.

AIKA BROWN, COMPOSITION WITH DOLLS, 1964.
MIXED MEDIA. COLLECTION ISRAEL MUSEUM.

He delivered young painting from its dignity and from the mysterious process of "making a painting" characterizing Impressionist Abstraction, inherited from the School of Paris. His feelings about the democratization of the means and materials of painting brought him to cover his works with posters and newspapers (after 1963), after a period of doodling and scribbling on and in the rosy, pink surface in a nonchalant, child-like automatism. Graffiti drawings on colour paintings on plywood, wall-paper, banal stereotypes, slogans and doodling phrases constitute his reaction to local art events, covering collages with automatic pencil drawings, all the while exhibiting the other quality which characterizes his style, his radical sensibility of colour painting. The inclusion of colour reproductions of world leaders (the Israeli chief-of-staff, Willy Brandt, etc.), and kitsch colour reproductions of sweet landscapes, mainly from the Seventies, are equivalents, in his works, to a coloured spot, to brush strokes. The sources of his early collage-paintings, in those of Rauschenberg (*Factum*, of 1957, for instance) appear obvious, but it is doubtful if in those years he had sufficient information about American art. It is more possible that the collages of square paper on acrylic of the mid-Seventies show a compositional influence of Hans Hoffman. Small labels on a richly coloured support bear, in handwritting, the word "head" and "geranium." These parodical-conceptual elements, may be reactions to the new epistemic art, widely shown in Israel during the early Seventies. His early paintings directly influenced the styles of Arie Aroch and Aviva Uri, in their openness and freedom of drawing, doodling, and scribbling. He represents "non-tradition," a subtle task in Tel-Aviv, where a building fifty years old is a historical sensation. The Tel-Aviv of his youth with its white houses in the bright sunlight, the white plaster peeled from the walls, the accepted standards of behaviour, all these elements provide a possible background to his characteristic style of *pittura povera*. These characteristics are even more pronounced in the works of his students (especially in their early phase) which bear his direct influence. Lavie's activity as a teacher is quite equal to his activity as painter and organizer. Among his disciples at the State Art Teachers Training College in Ramat-Hasharon, and elsewhere, one finds Garbuz, Nahum Tevet, Michal Na'aman, Tamar Getter and Tisibi Geva, and many others who compose the youngest generation on the local art scene. But unlike many of them, he never executed a work which can be defined as political. The choice of artists for the exhibitions of 10+, which lasted till 1971, was not dogmatic. It created a mood of experimentation and daring, and a few of the artists

RAFFI LAVIE, PAINTING, 1968-76.
COLLECTION GORDON GALLERY, TEL-AVIV.

PINCHAS ESHET, SUBJECT 13, 1966.
SHEET IRON.

who studied with Marino Marini at Milano's Brera Academy, showed in 1966 at the Tel-Aviv Museum thirty-three sheet-metal sculptures which bear a sensual expressionism in their representation of stylized body volumes, before passing in the Seventies to minimal and shaped canvases.

From the mid-Sixties onward, Uri Lifschitz (born 1936 in a kibbutz) has been the leading spokesman of figurative expressionist painting. Although he took part in the last *New Horizons* exhibition, his works bore no relation to Israeli abstraction. In fact, Lifschitz was the only mature repesentational Expressionist on the Israeli art scene during the late Sixties and early Seventies. His paintings resemble those of Francis Bacon in their energy, their brushstrokes, and their effective colours. Existential concerns are reflected in his works by a dynamic contortion of the human figure, by grotesque cynism or humour. Writing and scribbling appear from his early works through the series done after Velasquez at the beginning of the Seventies. The idea of old master paintings as given objects and hence as suitable models for paintings, is exemplified by Lifschitz in his Millet paintings. In the early Seventies the paintings of the American-born Ivan Schwebel, a self-educated virtuoso, done in a Velasquez-like expressionistic style, began to win recognition in the art circle. In the mid-Seventies, a new version of Bacon-expressionism is demonstrated by Youval Yariv. In his *White Fears* canvases, human bodies are arrested and distorted by mechanical instruments and roulette discs while women's wombs are replaced by meat mincers. His bitter social criticism was channelled in 1980 into paintings-as-political-protests, as he painted over large Rentgen films images of prime-ministers in negative.

Herald Rubin immigrated to Israel from South Africa, after being arrested there for anti-government activity. His paintings, bitter and ironic, are expressionistic statements against war and religious organs.

While 10+ carried on their colourful activity, the Helena Rubinstein Pavilion, built in the Habima National Theatre and Philharmonic complex in Tel Aviv, hosted annual "Salon D'Automne" exhibitions, up till 1969. In the large space of the pavilion, the

involved tried to assimilate late pop influences in their works. Yoav Barel, an art critic who shifted art writing, till then only vaguely professional, onto a serious theoretical path, experimented during the late Sixties with nudes, following an approach similar to that of Wesselman. Mitchel Baker, a new arrival from the United States, was like a living bridge of information about recent developments in the far-away art centre. He showed graphically oriented paintings. Every work bearing new figuration was defined in this circle as pop. This label was also applied to the fresh graphic work of Gad Ullman, the effective coloured erotism of Ran Schechori, Michael Druks's *Venus,* and the painted collages of Yair Garbuz. Aika Brown, interested in Tàpies's style, created black-tar assemblage-paintings, combining ropes and heads of puppets to create an expressionistic, surreal imagery. The young artists most involved in the events of the Seventies who made their first appearance in 10+ were Garbuz, Michael Druks and Yocheved Weinfeld. The group also included the gifted ceramic-scultor Ziona Shimshi (then still a painter) and Tuvia Beeri, the master etcher who studied with John Friedlander in Paris. Pinchas Eshet,

ACHIAM, PREGNANT WOMAN, c. 1960. BASALT.   SHLOMO SELINGER, ARCHAIC FIGURE, c. 1962.

ITZHAK DANZIGER, SHABAZYA, 1939.
NUBIAN SANDSTONE.

joyous mood of 10+ accounted for much of the new spirit in Israeli art. Alima, Mati Bassis, Hayuta Bàhat, exposed radically expressionistic abstracts, but in the 1969 Salon D'Automne, as in the spring show at the Artists House in Jerusalem, it became clear that Israeli art had reached a phase typical of the Seventies, characterized by conceptual and concrete art, epistemic drawing, political art, art in nature, process art, performances.

The student riots of 1968 skipped over Israel, still stunned by the Six Days war of June 1967. The small besieged state occupied a territory that extended from the Suez Canal to the gates of Damascus, from the sea across the hills of Judea and Samaria to the Jordan. Euphoria was the prevalent sensation, but for a small part of the population, this was a moment for moral introspection, for contemplation of the past history of "life by the sword," of an everlasting anxiety of war. The need to clear up the confusion, to study and implement the new reality, to understand and investigate the logic of existence in Israel, gave rise to a new artistic attitude, expressed by deserting the aesthetic of the art object. This tendency, later accelerated by the turmoil of political and existential awareness following the 1973 war, defined the main bulk of the art in Israel throughout the late Sixties and the Seventies. This art reveals two trends, which are interlocked, parallel, and simultaneous: one is political, mythological, and embraces earth works, conceptual, behavioural, and body art and their derivatives; the second is "new drawing" or the Epistemic Abstraction, as Robert Pincus-Witten defines it: "The term comes from the world 'epistemology,' the science of knowledge. Just as the realist ratified his work to be correct through a comparison between the thing in nature and its illusionistic counterpart in art, so too does the 'epistemic' abstractionist possess a system of ratification; only the comparison takes place not between nature and art, but between certain absolute ideas and art. These 'epistemic ideas' are as concrete and ratifiable as empirical knowledge gained from sensory stumuli" (from *On Neustein*, in the catalogue, Tel-Aviv Museum, July '77). I try to suggest here, that even such an esoteric art activity, which is conscious of the intimate questions of the logics of art and its processes, had in Israel political roots. Almost all the artists who dealt with epistemic drawing simultaneously executed political-mythological works. Such is the case with Neustein, Gershuni, Efrat, Kadishman, Ullman, Cohen Gan and others. Indeed, as was mentioned above, the founding of art in Palestine at the begining of the century was an act within the frame of the Zionist utopia and activity. Thus I defined the rise of the "Canaanitic" cultural movement for artistic creation, based on an ancient He-

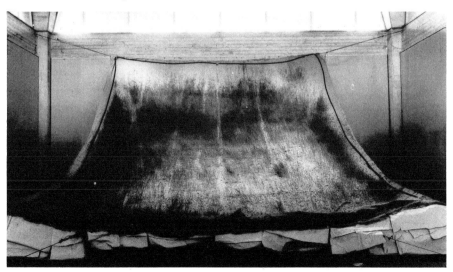

ITZHAK DANZIGER, SEEDED CANVAS, 1971. GROWTH ON PLASTIC EMULSION
COURTESY ISRAEL MUSEUM, JERUSALEM.

brew foundation, as a political struggle for the identity of the new Israeli nation. Also political were the concepts of the New Horizons abstractionists regarding the cultural image of society in the new-born state. By "political art" I mean the very characteristic creation which has manifested itself in Israel from the '67 war to the present, which is, first of all, based on deep concerns about identity and existence in this particular place; an art which seeks for roots, through personal and historical myths and through a particular connection to the earth on which two nations, the Israeli-Hebrew and the Palestinian-Arab, carry on a continuous bitter struggle for the right to exist. In this context, the most meaningful artistic creation, possibly the most "Israeli," is associated with the name of Itzhak Danziger.

An artist and teacher, Danziger remains the influential figure in the realm of art that looks for roots in the culture of the ancient East and in the concept of nature as artistic expression. Danziger did not believe in "productivity" in art. He created few objects and realized few projects. Each of them, however, had immense impact, radiating his feelings about culture, nature and justice. Born in 1927 in Berlin, he arrived as a child in Palestine where his father become a pioneer of

medicine. After studying sculpture at the Bezalel School in Jerusalem, with Zeev Ben-Zvi, and then at the Slade School of Fine Arts in London, he returned to Tel-Aviv and created, in 1939, his sculpture, *Nimrod,* described above. From the same reddish sandstone he executed in the same year a head of a woman, *Shabazya,* which combines two sources. The first is a Yemenite immigrant, a neighbour of his in Tel-Aviv, which bears the physiognomy of this remote Jewish tribe. The second source is the Mesopotamian style of a culture that existed three thousand years ago. Although not involved in the militant activity of the Young Hebrews, or Canaanites, he became an idol in their circles. Opposed and sharply criticized by the Zionist establishment in Palestine, the Canaanites and their periodical, "Aleph," as well as Danziger, were seen as a danger to Zionist homogeneity in those turbulent years of world war and of mass immigration of Jews to the newborn state. They were accused of paganism, of reviving archaic Canaanitic cults and rituals. They were isolated by the components of the Israeli community, from the nationalists and religious, to the ruling socialists. During the Forties, with an interruption in 1946 in which he studied with Ossip Zadkine in Paris, Danziger started to investigate phenomena char-

JOSHUA NEUSTEIN, REMOVAL, 1973.
LACQUER ON PAPER.

acteristic of the landscape of Palestine. These investigations resulted in his sheep sculptures, which combined Beduin tents, hills in the desert area, and the sheep who live in this environment. The sheep, said Danziger, are wandering sculpture. Danziger's sheep sculptures can be seen as a landscape of craters, water and hills. Marcel Janco defined them in the late Fifties as "topographic maps." His desert Negev sheep is titled *The Lord is My Shepherd* to emphasize the connection with archaic biblical culture.

Impressed by the enclosures and water reservoirs of the Bedouins, he made in the Fifties his "landscape structures," small forms done in bronze, wax or clay. He intended to make provisional sculptures, or works which would bear a feeling of the temporary, like nature itself. It is worth mentioning the remote but deep affinity between Danziger's point of view on archaic forms and that of Rudi Lehmann, the Berlin-born (1901) sculptor, who from his arrival in Palestine in 1933, till his death in 1977, was active as an artist and an influential teacher (his pupils included Kadishman, Tumarkin, Eshet). His small animal sculptures convey a simple yet monumental feeling, the origin of which lies in the animal sculptures of the ancient East, mainly those of pharaonic Egypt. Lehmann's rude, direct and nondecorative art, based on basic geometrical forms, was inherited by his pupils.

Itzhak Danziger was not a fanatic about keeping nature "pure" from human intervention. He said, "There are forms in nature, made by men, without which the landscape is not complete." But his largest project, *The Rehabilitation of the Nesher Quarry* (1971) was the correction of an area on the slopes of Mount Carmel, between the Haifa Bay and

JOSHUA NEUSTEIN, DISPLACEMENT, 1970.
ASPHALT AND HAY BALES.
RUBENSTEIN PAVILION, TEL-AVIV.

the mountains, whose ecological equilibrium had been destroyed by years of extensive quarrying of limestone for use in the cement industry. With the advice of a team of scientists from the Technion in Haifa, the damaged walls of the quarry were prepared to be covered with plastic emulsion in a beehive-like network, in which the emulsion would serve as artificial soil for the growth of vegetation.

The occasion of examining the growth of seeds in this plastic-emulsion imitation earth in a museum exhibition of historical importance was afforded by the *Concepts+Information* show, which opened at the Israel Museum, in Jerusalem, in February 1971 (the Museum of Modern Art in New York opened its first conceptual exhibition, *Information*, in July 1970). Danziger participated in this show with a surface suspended by cables in the hall; on it was spread the plastic emulsion, in which seeds might grow to create a suspended "arti-

② sol lewitt   ④ daniel buren   ③ gilbert and george   ① john baldessari

BENI EFRAT, A DRAWING COMPOSED OF LINES AND WORDS
WHICH WERE SENT TO THE ARTIST BY FOUR ARTISTS, 1973.

JOSHUA NEUSTEIN, PICTURE PLANE,
A PHOTOGRAPHIC STRATEGY (DETAIL), 1973.

ficial landscape," a functional ·work-in-process.

This exhibition included information about one of the first large-scale projects to combine a conceptual approach and a work in nature. It was the *Jerusalem River Project* executed the previous year by Joshua Neustein, with Battle and Marx, involving the invention of a make-believe river, using the medium of sound. Along two kilometers of a dry mountain valley situated to the east of Jerusalem toward the Judean desert, the recorded sound of streaming waters was distributed along the valley by fifty-five loudspeakers set on the ground. This expression of a nonexistent reality was accompanied by the authors' description: "There is an unconscious as well a real need for a wet element in the landscape of Jerusalem. In the Bible, on ancient maps, and in the folklore of the town, a river is shown or mentioned. Again and again, references can be found to a river that should be and is not." In the same year (1970), Neustein displaced, in the Rubinstein Pavilion of the Tel-Aviv Museum, a landscape with a piece of road and bales of hay. Neustein was born in Danzig (1940), educated in New York, and settled in Jerusalem in 1964. He worked with Arie Aroch and Mairovich, and began his intensive activity, mainly in the field of epistemic drawing, in 1968, stimulated by a work of Aroch where a line of folded paper was defined as a drawn line. His variations of drawings as cut, torn, crumpled, removed and replaced paper continued until the Eighties. At the same time, Beni Efrat worked with bent and folded paper, and covered with white paint a grid on white

paper, as though erasing it by drawing (*Adding to Substract*, 1970). Together, they formed the core of New Drawing in Israel, although in 1968 Moshe Gershuni showed a stain on paper made by melted butter. Those were the days of innovations achieved by examining the meaning of line as a material and the paper as an independent agent. Beni Efrat, in his sophisticated works, devoted all his efforts to concrete art. His *In-on-through* work on paper makes the linguistic definition concrete, by pressing in the word "in," by printing the word "on" on the paper, and by cutting through the world "through." His exhibition in the Israel Museum in February 1972 represented a radical approach to concrete-minimal concepts. The physical and chemical qualities of heavy sheet-metal in the process of rusting, the nonillusionistic representation of "real facts," became his contribution to "truth."

Two years later he executed a work which was to surpass all endeavours of Israeli Lyrical Abstraction: to represent the qualities of local light. In his *Fadings* Efrat exposed to the sunlight an industrially dyed, folded canvas, for twenty-four days. Each day, another part of the canvas was exposed, so that the gradual fading of the dye bears the effect of the sunlight on the canvas from an exposure ranging from one to twenty-four days. Efrat's nonillusionistic works replace emotional interpretation with physical facts and processes. Another project, in which Efrat dealt with art politics, was the exchange by mail of the words, lines and forms sent to him by more than a hundred artists in Israel and abroad in answer to his request, "Would you please exchange these lines for one of yours, to be used in a drawing." His work, combined from four artists' lines and words (Baldessari, Sol LeWitt, Gilbert & George, Daniel Buren), shown at the Gordon Gallery in Tel-Aviv in 1973, was done as an "experiment of experiments and experiences."

Efrat, who worked in London from the late Sixties to 1977, and thereafter in New York, in the last few years has mainly done film-performances (concerned with the juxtaposition of the two-dimensional medium of film, and live performance). In the show *Beyond Drawing,* in the Israel Museum in 1974, a show which summarized and announced the importance of epistemic and experimental drawing in Israel, Efrat exhibited the "spiral line," which does not exist but is created in our conscious by observing photographs of eyes looking along the unphotographed spiral. This show, which was seen as crucial in defining the existence of an Israeli trend in the Seventies, also included the *Picture Plane* of Joshua Neustein.

Neustein's concerns about art strategies ("If process is the subject of my art, what is its predicate?") is well expressed and performed in this work, which in twenty-four photos represents a process of creation. Here the major issues confronting the artist of the Seventies are posited: the relation between pictorial surface and support structure, the Wittgensteinian problem of context, and the resultant mad chase of perception in hunt of the object. Paint flows on folds in the paper and the artist penetrates beyond the picture frame. Shadows fall on torn fragments of paper pasted on the wall, so that one can not readily distinguish the limit of the line, the edge of the paper, or the limit of the experience. "Art is behaviour and not a product." This declaration by Neustein, made in relation to his picture plane, lead one to the political projects which he carried out as a parallel to his epistemic drawings. His concept of cut, removed and replaced drawings is also found in his *transplanted landscapes,* for examples the asphalt road and hay-bales he installed in the Tel-Aviv Museum. His first project was shown in 1969 (with G. Battle). He stuffed seventeen thousand old military boots into the Jerusalem Artists House. The boots,

**AVITAL GEVA, THE BOOKS PROJECT.
ART AS A SOCIAL SERVICE, 1972.** ON THE ROAD BETWEEN ARAB VILLAGE AND A KIBBUTZ.

brought from a junkyard near the old city of Jerusalem, conquered two years previously by the Israeli army, bear connotations of the wars in the area. The "hills" of heavy shoes, moving under the steps of the visitors, with the sound of an army marching in the background, comprised the earliest of the political projects which became characteristic of artistic activity in Israel during the Seventies.

Most of the artists who took part in this activity showed together from 1969 to 1972, in such shows as *Stop Green* and *Five Rooms* at the Artists House in Jerusalem, *Concept +Information* at the Israel Museum, and *Affidavit: Idea, Process, Document,* the exhibition of six Israeli artists held at the Gallery House in London. But the most meaningful meeting occured in the creative seminars which took place over a period of some months in the valley between a kibbutz,

Metzer, and the Arab village Messer, where Avital Geva's kibbutz is situated. In the early Seventies Geva became one of the more important young artists to deal with socio-political messages in the language of conceptual, behavioural and earth art. His social experience as a member of a socialist commune, and as a neighbour to Arab villages, led him to concentrate on the meaning of "the social ties of the Population." In his conceptual work *Environment Experiment,* 1971, he executed a yellow strip from the main street of his kibbutz to the main road to Tel-Aviv. Another strip in yellow was drawn from the highway entrance to the Israel Museum in Jerusalem. He defines this project as "a choice of an isolated area so as to connect it with the country's highway network. The yellow strip impresses the fact of distance. The observer feels through it the presence of the settlement and its location, and is more deeply aware of its isolated character." Avital Geva's Book projects became his best known instances of "art as social service." Under an agreement with paper mills situated in his area, thirty tons of old books, regarded as waste paper, were brought by the industry's trucks and spread along the main valley road, between the Arab villages and kibbutz settlements.

Geva defined this action as "an opportunity to transform a garbage-and waste-pile into a cultural and educational event," as the books were collected by the heterogeneous population, thus symbolizing possible ties between the two nations settled on the same land.

Typical of the Israeli political version of earth works, is the project by Micha Ullman, executed during the Metzer meetings in 1972, one year before the Yom-Kippur War. Ullman dug two identical trenches, one in the earth of Kibbutz Metzer, the other in the Arab village, Messer. Then he exchanged the earth from one to the other, to symbolize an "earth covenant" based on the traditional "blood covenant" of the East. This combination of trenches and ritual is as closely related to current existential and socio-political problems in Israel, as the mounds he erected in 1980 at the entrance to the Museum in Jerusalem and facing the hill of the Parliament (entitled *Till Here)* are related to concepts of cultural deterioration.

Since 1969 Micha Ullman has been intensively preoccupied with the examination of the concept of nature. At first his interest was manifested in an elaborate drawing of nature, which sought to discover a natural visual system of growth and of the establishment and

MICHA ULLMAN, TILL HERE, 1980.
EARTH AND CEMENT. THE ISRAEL MUSEUM, JERUSALEM.

DISENGOFF HOUSE. THE TEL-AVIV MUSUEM FROM 1932.

THE TEL-AVIV MUSEUM. OPENED IN 1971.

distribution of order. Later he began to work with the matter of nature itself. He dug out the earth, sorted it, and then gradually developed what turned out, at the end of the seventies, to be his goal: the construction of shelters, trenches, and mounds. These works brought together two courses of action. On one hand, the use of earth as a material and as an artistic metaphor; and on the other, the use of earth structures as a figurative expression of the lessons one learns about the human condition in society. Looking at Ullman, one immediately thinks of man digging himself in, out of an urgent need for self-protection. Such entrenchments, made of earth and reinforced by concrete, reflect the motto of Beckett's works: be sure to take shelter before you are hunted. The shelters and defense-pits convey an acute political sensation that is not typical of any specific geographical region. It is, rather, an existential sensation of traumatic fear, the assertion of the instinct of survival when confronted with oppressive powers. Ullman's fortifications are based on models that are very well known in his environment. His generation grew up surrounded by military entrenchments and shelters, and is well acquainted with wars and the fears that dwell inside personal pits. The earth-

sculptures he plants in his environment assimilate quite well with functional defense-systems and are not unlike excavations that reveal an ancient civilization which time has covered with layers of earth, as if to protect it from the hardships of the modern age.

Ullman's ascetic aesthetic is introverted, and though it could be defined as minimalistic, its message is directed away from the realm of art toward the reaction to socio-political situations. Though his syntax is indeed that of earth-art, his concrete works try to give shape to shapeless sensations that are derived from the experience of indentifying trenches with hiding, and shelters with fear. Says Ullman, "The anticipation of disaster sharpens the consciousness of it." Ullman creates an environment charged with attentiveness and anticipation, which acts as an intermediary between frightened man and nature.

Moshe Gershuni is mentioned above as one of the first artists who dealt in Israel with conceptual art and epistemic drawing. His questioning works concerning art materials were displayed as early as 1969 at the Israel Museum. A sheet of white paper painted black at the edges, was entitled *The paper is white outside, but black inside.* A graphite

MICHA ULLMAN, TRENCHES (DETAIL), 1980.
EARTH. INSTALLATION AT THE VENICE BIENNALE.

אבי , צבי גרשרני , עלה לארץ בשנה 1929 .

נטע פרדסים וכרפיס .

MOSHE GERSHUNI, MY FATHER IMMIGRATED TO PALESTINE IN 1929.
PLANTED GROVES, 1974. PHOTOGRAPH WITH RED COLOR.

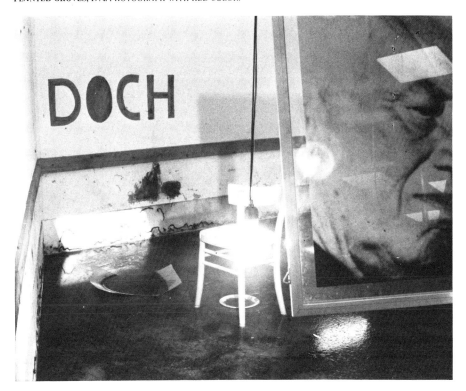

MOSHE GERSHUNI, RED SEALING/THEATRE (DETAIL), 1980.
INSTALLATION AT THE VENICE BIENNALE.

line on paper "asked" if it was drawn in profile or frontally. These works were followed by close-up photographs of the artist's mouth, tongue and toes. Gershuni questioned the meaning of the art product, and proceeded to examine the body while probing his own personal myths. He touched on such national myths as immigration and settlement, and the transplanting of culture in (an interest shared with other artists, notably Cohen Gan). The image of his father, an Eastern European intellectual who became a citrus grower in his new homeland, gave rise to questions about the connection between deep-rooted local culture and immigrant culture. Dealing with issues of culture and society, Moshe Gershuni's works engender intense feelings and acute sensations, and they try, as he says, to establish themselves "on the border between the sublime and the ridiculous." His works, which may bring to mind the concepts of Arte Povera, make permanent use of ordinary, insignificant everyday words and objects. His struggle against cultural and political coercion has resulted in works like *Benedictus*, 1974, in which behind black curtains he quoted texts such as the Agnus Dei, which were prohibited in the educational system in his school days, especially in the religious wing where he was educated. This issue of the perpetual cultural struggle for and against the image of Israel as a Jewish state, where traditional religious laws constitute the only legal system, was rarely touched on by the political artists of the Seventies. One finds again Michael Druks's *Eastward Contemplation*, 1977, in which the artist performed the daily ritual of phylactery prayer replacing the holy object with cameras and straps. Another young artist who remembers with self-pity his religious education is Motti Mizrahi, who repeated Jesus' journey along the Via Dolorosa with his own portrait on his back. In this symbolic performance, he identified his own physical sufferings and political situation with those of Jesus. Mizrahi said: "This is a story about a man in Eretz-Israel who paid for people's reaction to what he had said. Jesus' sufferings are mine."

Gershuni's perception of the artist as an outsider who poses disturbing questions, and his practice as an influential teacher, and citizen who never ceased to criticize the authorities, were accompanied by political posters against government policy (after the 1977 elections), with the participation of Geva, Ullman and Tumarkin; and by direct political works. His 1979 installation in the Julie M. Gallery, a Tel-Aviv gallery which has supported the local avant-garde since the mid-Seventies, reproduced an investigation-room in which individual freedom is jeopardized. The use of thick red paint emphasizes the traumatic experience of war in his works. The question written on the walls, "Who is a Zionist and who is not," reflects the atmosphere of nationalism in Israel. At the 1980 Venice Biennale, Gershuni created a bloody, expressive environment *(Red Sealing / Theatre),* where thick red paint was used to seal cracks and corners, as if to close off and isolate a trapped site. Rain water, entering through openings in the ceiling, accumulated in a reservoir whose red walls and bottom gave the water the appearance of blood. Gershuni dealt here with a desperate image of his homeland, and complicated the anxiety by posing crucial questions about its cultural identity and its ambiguity between "true" Levantine culture and the acquired culture of the West.

Michael Druks, who showed with 10 + during the late Sixties, had an environmental exhibition at the Israel Museum in 1970, and in the same years exhibited a section of poster-layers from a municipal poster board in Tel-Aviv. This found object included a "recent archeology" of town events. In *Concept+Information* at the Israel Museum, he made a photo-montage in which the chimney of an electric power station appeared as a canon. In 1971 Druks began his *Flexible Geography* series, in which he folds and models maps of the world to obtain a personal geography, folding the map of Switzerland, for instance, to make an island. *Druksland*, a collage of a socio-physical map in the form of the artist's portrait, bears the phrase, "Occupied Territory." His direct political approach, which includes the *Communication Distrurbances* series begun in 1972 (in which hands and objects disturb the images of leaders on the television screen) parallels epistemic, conceptual, and video works.

Since 1972, Pinchas Cohen Gan has con-

MICHAEL DRUKS, OPINION, 1978.

tributed to the contemporary art scene in Israel with a wide range of activities, from socio-political projects, to conceptual work and painting, to the suggestion of non-Euclidian geometry. Cohen Gan was born in Meknes, Marocco in 1942, and arrived in Israel seven years later. This fact was to be of crucial importance, as his *Activities* of 1972-74 dealt with the problem of identity. As an immigrant who was transplanted from his natural environment onto new soil, he questions the possibility of the new environment becoming a natural one. On a personal-existential level he attacked the national political question of the possibility of Israel to integrate with the geopolitical reality which surrounds it. As if to symbolize these problems, his *Activities* (documented at the Israel Museum in 1974), included an experiment in the Dead Sea, in which no organism can live.

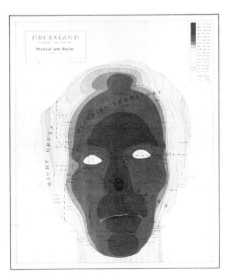

MICHAEL DRUKS, DRUKSLAND, 1974.
COLLAGE.

Fish were piped into the salt water in polyethylene tubes, connected at one end to a source of fresh water. "As the salinity of the waters increased with the growing distance from the fresh water source, and as life and salinity are in inverse ratio to each other," he commented, "the possibility of existence declines with the growing distance from the source." A tragic conclusion about the possibility of the cultural integration of immigrants in their new homeland. Again to illustrate the problem of the integration of Israel in its environment, he diluted two gallons of water from the Dead Sea into the meeting-point of the Pacific and

Neustein called this project *Maa(n)ses*, which is a yiddish word meaning something between fable and action, usually taken from everyday life, and containing hefty nuances of exaggeration. Neustein defined himself as a refugee till 1964 (the year of his arrival in Jerusalem from New York). The next political activity of Cohen Gan was *Touching the Border*, (shown in photos in the exhibition dedicated to "Borders" at the Israel Museum in 1980). The action entailed four Israeli citizens travelling toward the four borders, and marking the points where they were stopped by the army by burying lead bars stamped with demo-

PINCHAS COHEN GAN, FROM "THE DEAD SEA PROJECT", 1972-73.

Indian Oceans, near the Cape of Good Hope in South Africa. In one exhibition photographs were shown of the tent which Cohen Gan installed in a Palestinian refugee camp near Jericho in order "to express the feeling of a man who is in the situation of a permanent refugee". This project was realized a few months after the 1973 war, which shocked Israeli society, and caused a traumatic reevaluation of some basic concepts of existence, power, and peace in the light of the unsolved conflict. The refugee art of Cohen Gan reminds one of the large mail-art project that Joshua Neustein realized in 1972. Neustein sent artists (Beuys, Serra etc.) information about their works presented as his work.

graphic information. "A border is marked on maps as an internal line, and its marking is a visual, graphic sign. The limit of our strength is not a geographic border, but . . . a border between cultures, the distance between them being much greater than the geographical distance." "The border between the populations of Jerusalem is equivalent to the border between the communities in Israel. Touching the border poses a question," observes Cohen Gan. Around 1975 he shifted toward painting in a search for a new logic, code, and formula for dealing the with impossibility of painting to represent data and images. His coloured paintings from the last five years deal with the human figure as a scale, and with naïve,

NAHUM TEVET, INSTALLATION FOR CITY UNIVERSITY, NEW YORK, 1980-81.
WOOD, STEEL, OIL PAINT.

MICHAEL GITLIN, FROM THE "4' x 8'" SERIES, 1974-75. WOOD.

ironic, or parodic approaches to science and its application in art.

In the second third of the Seventies one finds in New York a selective colony of Israeli artists, most of them advocates of epistemic abstraction. Their encouragement in this centre, as contemporary artists and the existence of an Israeli art gallery (Bertha Urdang) who backed them, made their stay there possible. The acceptance of Buky Schwartz's video projects and Beni Efrat's film-performances by the Whitney Museum, make the sojourn of Israeli artists in New York an ongoing phenomenon. Neustein, Gitlin, Cohen Gan, Ben Haim and Doktori keep their Israeli identity by frequent shows in Israel, while living aboard, as do Druks (in London), Shlomo Koren (Amsterdam), and those veteran artists who have lived in Paris since the beginning of the Fifties, like Avigdor Arikha and Yaacov Agam.

Two artists who won attention from the begining of the Seventies, Michael Gitlin and Nahum Tevet, use an epistemic language to create, mainly, indoor installations. Michael Gitlin deals with the concept of the whole and its disintegration. His black-painted wooden plates are cut and displaced, to be re-integrated in the conscious of the spectator, in the process of perception.

Within the discipline of Postminimalism, his works act as markers of a given space, while keeping the gesture of the hand, splitting the wood which bears a strong tactile feeling. Gitlin's works, shown also in Documenta 1977 (where six other Israeli artists were represented: Karavan, Neustein, Efrat, Cohen Gan, Druks and Kadishman) bears a strong affinity to the Concrete Art of Beni Efrat and to the torn-removed-deplaced drawings of Neustein.

Nahum Tevet's indoor wood installations act as a transparent space within a given space. A twin-like linear construction on rounded bases deals with the analysis of perception, with the confrontation of memory versus identification. The multiple construction, built as a three-dimensional "concrete drawings," radiates a feeling of stress, of a search for an outlet. These "drawing-sculptures" resulted from a long series of drawings, which range from research about

spatial concepts from Malevitch to Bochner. Beginning in 1971 with an Israeli version of "poor" objects, Tevet created, after the '73 war, series of minimal airplane-like structures, with hidden planes of painting.

In 1972 Menashe Kadishman returned to Israel, after a ten-year stay in London. He undertook a cycle of works, beginning with works influenced by the rocks of the Israeli desert, and subsequently moving on to mythological images of the ancient East, minimal sculpture, environmental projects, conceptual works, personal and cultural mythologies, and "new painting." Born in Tel-Aviv in 1932, he studied with the legendary sculptor and teacher Rudi Lehmann, through whom he became conscious of primary, bold, earthy forms impregnated with a sense of the ancient East. In 1959 he enrolled at the St. Martin School of Art in London, where, together with Buky Schwartz and alongside Anthony Caro, he witnessed the development of English minimal sculpture, later creating minimal sculptures of his own which resemble nongravitational masses, as seen in his urban sculpture *In Suspense*, in Tel-Aviv (1967-74). Kadishman's most famous recent contribution to art in Israel is his *Sheep Project*, shown at the Israeli Pavilion of the 1978 Venice Biennale, where the artist applied art concepts to nature and adopted natural concepts as art concepts.

Kadishman introduced a flock of living sheep into the Israeli Pavillion—a segment of real life with the processes involved in it—as the realization of an idea in the realm of art-strategy which is, in essence: nature as a material, a theme and a process of art. This is an art which points at and delimits a situation of nature; a demonstrative rather than a descriptive art. "Perhaps the tension between constraint and freedom is the core of Kadishman's intention," wrote Paul Wember in his introduction to the artist's show *Concepts and Their Realization* in 1971 at the Museum Haus Lange, Krefeld, "Constraint: the principle of nature; freedom: the principle of art."

By choosing sheep as the theme and the material of his art, Kadishman attempts to turn to the primary and the simple, to strike a balance between an aesthetic, emotional form and personal experiences which are related to

MENASHE KADISHMAN, FLOCK OF SHEEP, 1980.
OIL ON CANVAS. COLLECTION GOTTESMAN.

a time and a place, as reference points in one's own geography and biography. Kadishman goes back to the time when he was a shepherd in an agricultural kibbutz in the Valley of Jezreel. He says: "I want my work to exercise all the senses." Kadishman's staining of the wool on the sheep's backs with blue, reminds one that flocks of sheep in the Middle East are stained with color as a shepherd's code, just as they had been marked with stars and crescents in ancient Assyria. In the caves of the Judean desert, facing the Dead Sea, explorations have brought to light relics of texts and objects that had belonged to the militant Jewish opponents of Roman rule. Among these were found blue-painted fleeces which had had a mythical-ritualistic significance.

The painting of nature *in situ*, as Kadishman has painted the back of the sheep, tallies with his painting of nature carried out in the past. On the surface of the brown earth of the Valley of the Cross in Jerusalem which lies at the foot of the hill where the Israel Museum is located, he painted in 1975 a square with a bright yellow colour. The brown clods of earth substituted in this "environmental painting" the canvas of traditional painting, while the angle of view enabled the eye to incorporate into it also the rocks and the old olive trees that surrounded the painted area.

Uphill, in the Museum garden, in the 1972 exhibition, *Landscape-Abstraction-Nature* in 1972, he painted a tree with yellow, as a landscape painting within the landscape itself. The eternity of the art product has been substituted here for the ephemeral quality determined by the power of the tree to assimilate the colour that had temporarily turned it into a painting. All this extends the confrontation between a fact of nature and a fact of sculpture which Kadishman carried into effect in the first version of *The Forest* project at the International Symposium of Sculpture in Montevideo at the end of the 1960s. Kadishman attached rectangular yellow metal plates to the trunks of trees in order to create "a forest within a forest," as he put it. The organic forms, the eucalyptus trees and the man-made angular technological forms intermingled to define "an artistic space" within the given space of nature. The straight-angled metal plates painted in industrially pigmented yellow, seemed as if they had come out of a Mondrian painting in order to hover in three dimensions within the colours of nature. The trees' branches and foliage were reflected as in a mirror on the surface of the shining plates, and produced shadows that changed constantly according to the angle of the sunlight. The yellow plates made the trees fall within the definition of art products, and the laws of nature adopted the artist's intervention-marks and incorporated them into the natural shadows of the forest.

The Forest, which constitutes an environmental work of "corrected nature," is an ex-museum project, and was presented in various versions: on the trees of New York's Central Park along Fifth Avenue, as part of Kadishman's show at the Jewish Museum in 1970 (Edward Fry wrote then, "Kadishman has established a perceptual and even pictorial situation in which his rectangular yellow planes act as disjunctive segments of an implicit, single picture plane"), and in his exhibition *Concepts and Their Realization* in the Haus Lange Museum in Krefeld in 1971.

The concept of aperture is further emphasized in the *Trees in Negative* projects which Kadishman has carried out from 76 and which elaborate on the "forest" theme.

In 1975, Kadishman set up *The Canvas Forest* on the grounds of the Israel Museum situated on a hill exposed to the winds. Canvas sheets (tarpaulin), six metres high, were hung on a cable structure. In the sheets he cut shapes of trees, like silhouettes, apertures in the form of trees through which one could see other aperture-trees and, through which the landscape was perceived. Kadishman set up here a metaphorical forest having the proportions of real trees, so that the natural forces that work on a forest would work also on his cloth. The treatment of the exterior-interior issue (the visitors could actually walk through the tree-forms) is included in this project, as well as the introduction of a remote landscape into the spaces cut in the canvas, just like in Kadishman's "hovering" glass sculptures where the background landscape had been incorporated into the sculpture.

In the wake of *The Canvas Forest* and on the basis of the same principle, Kadishman "planted" in 1977 *Trees in Negative.* Eight metal plates, each about eight meters high, constitute a private forest through which one can see the landscape, the frame of which is the contour lines of the trees. The metal trees within the landscape take us back to Kadishman's early works, carried out in nature at the beginning of the 1960s. In one of these he filled a square hole with glass splinters ("in order," as he said, "that they should grow glass trees, in your imagination"); in another

he buried, amidst clods of earth in a field, a photograph of land that was as dry and cracked as the desert, as if in order to carry the Israeli desert—here he had travelled in his proto-sculptural days—everywhere he went. In his tendency toward the materialization of art by means of taking the metaphor back to its place in nature and applying artistic concepts to segments of real nature, Kadishman could not avoid pointing at a place and a form that are deeply rooted in his personal mythologies. The sheep with the blue stains on their woollen backs, are the realization of this tendency, which is essentially a turning from metaphor and illusion toward observation and concrete contact with nature itself.

After the *Telephone Pages* of 1970, which Kadishman conceived as a travel diary of his experience as a wandering artist, he started after 1978 to paint huge unstretched canvases with the obsessive theme of sheep. His colourful, wild, intuitive paintings can be seen as a meaningful contribution to the wave of new painting, although he has no interest in painting trends, or painting theory, other than that expressed by the obsessive repetition of the sheep-image as a code to his roots in Eretz-Israel.

Revealing the myths that exist in the culture and nature of Israel became the artistic and socio-political goal of Itzhak Danziger, in an intensive period which lasted from the end of the 1973 war until his death, in 1977, in a car crash on the highway to Jerusalem. The Canaanitic concepts described above which led him to the creation of the mythic Nimrod, the sheep as a synthesis of living and natural forms, the investigations of the Nabatian, and Bedouin desert irrigation systems, and the rehabilitation of the quarried slopes of Mount Carmel, brought him to concentrate on the myth of the oak tree in the Galilee. He found that oaks sheltered and guarded the old Circassian Palestinian cemetery in the Galilee just as they guarded the isolated graves, hundreds of years old, of Jewish Rabbis. The oak guarded the cemetery, and the cemetery guarded the oak (in a region where, in five centuries of Turkish rule, all the old forests had been destroyed). He was astonished to find, in the Galilee mountains, evidence of an unknown ritual of oaks: sheets of green and blue cloth, hanging on oak branches. The cloths were clean, evidently replaced frequently. Burning coals around the site gave it a magnificent odour. There were no villages around and no road to climb the hill easily. Danziger said some weeks before his death, "The tree as an oracle exists in the belief of the are symbols of life and hope. No stain and no fold can be found on the cloths. I became obsessed with trying to understand these ancient rituals. I found in London a book edited in 1897, entitled, *The Tree and the Religious Myth*. It begins with the sentence, "the tree as an oracle exists in the belief of the Semitic race, and is expressed in the tradition of the Tree of Knowledge." The idea of the tree as a place, is emphasized in the history and tradition of Canaan. Danziger's investigations and journeys in the Galilee led him to find, in a remote area, Arab graves covered with bright cloths. Stitched around the covered grave between the black basalt stones, were fragments of flags, embroidered in gold with forms of the moon, Arabic caligraphy and handprints.

The point in Danziger's concern about local myths, is that in Israeli society, there are cultural (mythical and ritual) bonds to the earth and to the land which are obscure to the Israeli who comes back to his homeland in search of ties with its population and its tradition. From this viewpoint, it is easy to understand his struggle for the rights of the Palestinian Arabs to occupy their earth, to restore the signs of local culture, and to give up any attitude of power for the sake of coexistence. His inspiration of and influence on the generation of artists who, during the Seventies, espoused political or mythical earth concepts, have been described above. Danziger's last project was the replacement of a monument to the fallen by planting oak trees. Some months before the traumatic 1973 war, the Tel-Aviv Fund for the Arts invited Danziger, Kadishman, George Segal and Kenneth Noland to create sculptures in the city. Surprisingly, Segal decided to create the image of Abraham sacrifying Isaac. Concerning the project, he said, "After deciding about the subject of my work, I prepared myself by reading *Fear and Trembling* by Kirkegaard. In it are included five scripts; in each of them

the author imagines the sequence of Abraham's throughts while climbing with Isaac to Mount Moriah. I tried to reconstruct the personality and image of Abraham, then of Isaac: Did he obey or refuse? Then I reached the definite conclusion: Abraham did not sacrifice Isaac. He was, without doubt, a genius in preserving life. We do not have angels; we do not talk with God. We know that everything happens in our mind.

"Abraham was the first to break the tradition of sacrificing one's sons. His predecesors, as always, found many reasons to do it. But Abraham decided: Life is more important. He was very different from Jesus." George Segal saw this four months before the Yom-Kippur War.

In 1976 Joshua Neustein executed his last political project, the *Territorial Imperative,* in the Golan Heights. His metaphor of a dog urinating to fix his territorial imperative (a definition used by Disraeli in relation to the British colonies overseas) was realized *in situ,* in a new settlement. In its directness it is compared with the work of the young Michal Na'aman who wrote on a huge board, "The eyes of the state" fixing it on the shore. This saying was quoted from a television interview with a young soldier, in the 1973 war, who used the phrase in connection with the fall of

GEORGE SEGAL, ABRAHAM AND ISAAC, 1973.

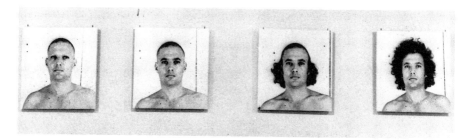

GIDEON GECHTMAN, PROCESS OF OPEN-HEART SURGERY (DETAIL), 1974.

an important Israeli radar station on the summit of Mount Hermon on the Syrian border. As in the case of the first generation of epistemic and political artists, she dealt simultaneously with these disciplines. In 1975 she focused her work on analogies between verbal and visual extensions. In a work presented in *Art en Garde,* 1975 (in the only number of this art magazine) Michal Na'aman performed with a line drawn along her body, which continued along a stretched string. The line changed with the movement of her body; rhymes so written in a sequence of photos were regarded as analogous to visual rhymes. Her postconceptual work in the second half of the Seventies, dealing with words and pictures, time and space, led her gradually to sophisticated colour painting. Similarly, Tamar Geter shifted from verbal, conceptual, informative works about art, to correlative concepts of culture and myth (the Tel-Hai yard, symbolic of Israeli pioneering settlements, versus the ideal city of the Renaissance), and then to colour painting of superimposed archetypes.

The search into personal, cultural and socio-political myths, memories and subject matter gained momentum during the seventies and included the efforts of young artists as well as those of the generation who started to show in the Sixties. Ziona Shimshi, a leading ceramic-sculptor, devoted her work to parodical and humouristic art-as-play self-criticism of the Israeli mentality, moving skilfully from bold figurative volumes to decorative forms. Bianka Eshel-Gershuni created large-scale body-sculptures in artisan-jewelery methods, combining gold feathers and pearls in an exaggerated baroque style, which alternated toward the end of the seventies with arte-poveresque jewels made of found materials, tar, thick red paint, and micro-images of dead creatures.

Avner Katz expressed a desperate reality in humouristic macabre drawings and pointed sculptures, as did Maris Bishofs, newly arrived from Russia, in caricaturizing a crazy society and art circles, from a point of

EPHRAT NATAN, FLAG, 1976. PHOTOGRAPH.

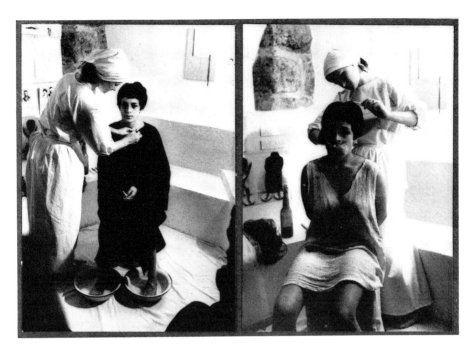

YOCHEVED WEINFELD, RITUAL PERFORMANCE, 1976.
PERFORMANCE AT THE DEBEL GALLERY, JERUSALEM.

MOTTI MIZRAHI, VIA DOLOROSA, 1973.

MOTTI MIZRAHI, RITUALS, 1977.

view which synthetises Sol Steinberg and Chaplin. More direct in his political and social approach is Yair Garbúz, a discipline of Raffi Lavie and teacher in the Art Teachers Training College in Ramat-Hasharon (a school from which a large part of the young artists who characterized art in Israel during Seventies came). His works from these years, collages of xeroxed paper on plywood, parodied society as a ridiculous crowd of fools in an orgy. Toward the middle of the decade, his combine-works were directed toward open criticism of local social truths and slogans. He demystified myths of immigration, the army, and Israeli national achievements. Using ludicrous language in his writings he mocked Hebrew cultural heroes.

The intense activity of young artists, free from definite styles and involved in the political situation, was summed up in 1976 by two shows: one, the *Open Workshop* at the Israel Museum, Jerusalem; the other, the performance meeting in Tel-Aviv, organized by the critic Gideon Ofrat. Direct political concerns ruled both events. Ester Schvarohman built during the workshop a typical Arab dwelling of mud and straw. In the same month, she executed in front of the Tel-Aviv Museum a performance dealing with the symbols and myths of Palestine, using earth, olives, and lambs. Gabi and Sharon invited Arab workers from occupied territory in Judea to build a stone wall. Gideon Gechtman, who since the beginning of the Seventies has surprised the public with his body-art works, like exhibiting the complete process of his open-heart operation and the prodution of brushes from his own hair, during the workshop did a much-criticized work about using Arabs as second-class workers.

Moshe Gershuni, who participated in the performance meeting, repeated his obsessive vocal piece, singing a nostalgic Hebrew song from the twenties as a means of comparing the memory of the ideal society of that time, with the disillusion of the present situation.

In the same year, Yocheved Weinfeld performed a body-art piece (in the Debel Gallery in Jerusalem, which specialized in this field). The feminine content of her work was based on the behavioural dictates of the traditional code of Jewish law, which forces a detailed purifying process on women. The young Ephrat Natan used performances to invent rituals which convey meanings of border and death. Dganit Berest, in photos and combine-works, remained esoteric in her images of checking memory, and comparing forms and cultural signs. A more direct approach was followed by Chaim Maor, who in 1978 showed in the exhibition *Art-Society* organized by the young curator Sara Breitberg at the Tel-Aviv Museum (directed from 1977 by Marc Scheps, an ex-artist who showed in the

MICHAL NA'AMAN, THE EYES OF THE COUNTRY, 1974. PHOTOGRAPH.

beginning of the Sixties at the Nouveaux Realists' gallery "J" in Paris) a wrapped shirt on plywood, photo and words: "Whether it be thy son's coat?" as a result of a characteristic Israeli and Jewish social atmosphere recalling such concepts as "martyrdom" and "defense of the fatherland."

In opposition to most of the works concerned with political, social and mythological themes, a small body of artists—the Leviathan group composed mainly of Russian newcomers—called for a "national style, based on the constructive spirit of the state, on Zionism, and on Jewish mysticism." Another group, called Aklim (Climate) advocated after 1973 a return to landscape painting in order to create an Israeli art based on the characteristic light and colours of the place (hence, identical in aspiration to art in the twenties). Many interesting painters showed with this group, including Eliahu Gat, Ori Raizman and Michael Gross. Lilian Klapisch, who immigrated to Israel in 1970, executes saturated, painterly canvases, geometrically divided and cut in their structure (a result of her meeting with the "schizophrenic reality", as she said). In the spirit of Lyrical Abstraction, one finds the paintings of Shimon Avni; Shlomo Vitkin, remembered from the late Fifties for his Villon-like canvases, radicalized toward the nonobjective; and the white canvases of Arie Azen, intended to reveal the order in the denaturalized landscape.

Reminiscent of the short period of Israeli pop (mainly shown at the 10 + exhibitions in the Sixties), are the early works of Oded Feingersh, whose idiom is now poetic and desolate in expression. Michael Eismann endeavours to combine a style which recalls Dubuffet with innocent scribbling in order to reach a decorative result.

Mirit Cohen returned from New York to show in 1978 an environment of energetic, nervous contacts between wires and broken glass, an antithesis to the obsessive search for one possible true form by Yadid Rubin, who participated in the *Five Rooms* show in Jerusalem in 1969, filling a space with transparent containers. Minimalism and colour vibration were the goals of Reuven Berman's intellectualized canvases throughout the Sev-

ZIONA SHIMSHI, THE T.V. ICON, 1976. CLAY.

enties. Alima, toward the end of the decade, left her ascetic, reductive painting in favour of colourful, free drawing. Michael Argov progressed from abstract to white canvases, to monumental minimalism, and then to painting folds on the soft folds of the canvas itself.

The shift in style by experienced artists, toward the end of the Seventies, was caused by the urgent need for introspection under the stress and the moral, political, and social shock that followed the events of 1973. The

BIANCA ESHEL-GERSHUNI, GO BRIDE UNTO THY GROOM, 1983. COLLECTION TEL-AVIV MUSEUM.

results were always a search into the cultural and mythological roots of Israel and the Middle East. Neomi Smilansky, a master printmaker, created in 1978 her *Mediterranean Leaves*, which combine acquatint and intaglio to make a three-dimensional folded object, which recalls leaves and scrolls found in an archeological site in Palestine. Oriental architectural constructions are the latest result of the work of Israel Hadani who showed, in the 1972 Venice Biennale, polished minimal sculptures. His recent proposals of *Desert Sculptures* are an Israeli version of postmodern aesthetics.

painting is described above. Young painters, who create colourful figurative works, have gained appreciation, which could not have happened in the early seventies. Dorit Feldmann showed in 1980 combined works of colour photos and three-dimensional bodies. The effective colour and images create a vision of sensual radiation, of enigmatic organic curves and hints of mystery. Linda Zandhaus shifted from her writting-tachism pages toward expressionistic, wild, colourful energism. Ronit Eiger has built shaped canvases covered with bold decorative painting. Tisibi Geva, who executed ascetic "poor"

AVNER KATZ, UNTITLED, 1975. COLORED CLAY.

A kaleidoscopic view of art in Israel in 1980 reveals a possible shift toward painting, colourful and free from the limits of ruling trends. Moshe Gershuni, with a political motivation, burst forth around 1980 with red colour on paper to create signs of anger and despair, hand painted with words like: "Peace soldier, I am a soldier, mortal fear." The folded paper works of Neustein become, toward 1979, a support for effective colours; and Kadishman's shift toward colourful

sculptures, is creating his first suggestions of painted environments.

Shaul Schatz, remembered for his De Kooning-like etchings of 1970, appears again, but now with expressionistically colourful paintings; Yaacov Mishori represents, as part of the revival of colour painting, the wild expressionistic representational approach; recently, his "punk" aggressive portraits have replaced his ambivalent, sexual, photographic self-portraits. Osvaldo Romberg (in

Israel since 1973) represents analytical painting, or "painting as analysis of classical paintings" and as a didactic tool. His ambitious project *From Prehistory to Manet* was shown recently in the Tel-Aviv Museum. His works include reproductions of the analyzed painting, an analytic chart of the colours, and didactic writings. As Igal Zalmona writes, "The possibility offered by Romberg is the unification of interpretation and didactics (the language with the visual). Thus, visuality and iconography are strengthenend and legitimatized by language."

The contemporary art meeting, Tel-Hai '80, held in the Galilee in September of that year, provided an opportunity to summarize the main trends in art in Israel during the seventies. It was the first time that socialist equalitarian communes organized a project of contemporary art-in-nature, video, and performance. The decision to realize the project, with the participation of forty-two artists, was made by the members of the twenty-seven kibbutzim of the upper Galilee, part of which are situated on the borders of Syria and Lebanon. The site was in and around the historical park of Tel-Hai and the regional Art College of the kibbutzim. The central theme of the meeting was the execution of fixed works in the open, in relation to the dominant implications of the landscape

CHAIR MAOR, WHETHER IT BE THY SON'S COAT?, 1978. WRAPPED SHIRT ON PLYWOOD, PHOTOGRAPH AND LETTERS.

and to the historical and mythological meanings of the site. The artists approached nature as a subject rather than a model, as a material and as a spatial realm in which to build site-specific works of art.

Using basalt stones, Dalia Meiri built dome-like structures around the trunks of four olive trees. Like her previous works, executed from the mid-Seventies on, her recent work relates to nature, to personal myths, and quite noticeably, to archeology. She is familiar with the ancient primitive civilization which had used stone to produce winepresses, oil and mill stones. "It is possible," she said, "that sculptures of mine, erected in the field, will look like remnants of early tools that served the ancient inhabitants of the area, relics of the old civilization of the land of Israel." It seems that the concepts of Danziger found in Meiri a continuity. Her memorial, a

MICHAEL EISMANN, FROM THE ART DIARY BOOK, 1980. MIXED MEDIA ON PAPER.

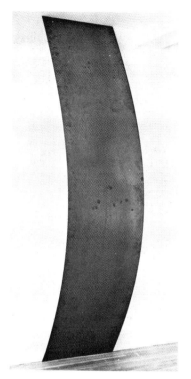

DGANIT BEREST, THE CIRCLE BESIDE VIRGINIA, 1976.
WOODEN SCULPTURE AND PHOTOGRAPH.
COURTESY JULIE M. GALLERY, TEL-AVIV.

SHLOMO KOREN, ARC, 1975.
STEELPLATE.

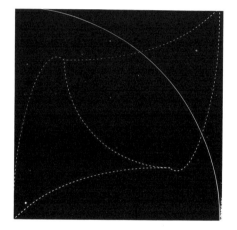

REUVEN BERMAN, ARCS DU CUBE A 90°, 1978.
ACRYLIC NO. 4 FROM 20 PANELS.

NEOMI SMILANSKY, MEDITERRANEAN LEAVES, 1978.

MICHAEL ARGOV, RELIEF, 1975.

MICHA LAURY, BEHIND/OVER, 1975.
LEAD, GLASS.

BOAZ VAADIA, BASALT SCULPTURE, TEL HAI, 1980.

TULLY BAUMAN, PRINT IN NATURE, TEL HAI, 1980.
SILKSCREEN ON BASALT AND LIMESTONE.

DALIA MEIRI, STONE SHELTERS AROUND OLIVE TREES, TEL HAI, 1980.

circle of local boulders, executed in her home settlement situated on the basalt heights, recalls works by Richard Long. Boaz Vaadia worked with the same natural materials. Having lived in New York during the previous five years, at Tel-Hai he built a pattern of basalt rocks, which looks like a relic of archaic agricultural or ritual constructions. Batia Arowetti related her work to the history of the site by installing a tent of pink satin on a structure of pink neon. The tent was set up on a site where Jewish poineers in the Galilee fought and fell. Arowetti used the pink satin and neon to create a spot of nostalgia from the standpoint of the present. Her indoor installations deal with images taken from the culture of the a ancient East.

Dov Heler, another young artist, a member of a kibbutz situated in the arid south of Israel, dealt with the phenomena of rain and drought. On the slope of the Tel-Hai hill he reconstructed garden terraces which were typical of the place in the past. Ezra Orion, who during the mid-sixties studied at the St. Martin School of Art in London (like Kadishman and Buky Schwartz) has concentrated his efforts in the last decade to plan a sculpture field near Sdeh Boker in the Negev, where he lives. This "total sculpture" project, as large as a town, fits his concepts as he describes them: "Sculpture has to be way above the size of humans. Tens of metres high. Extending over hundreds of square metres. Sculpture has to dominate the entire space that contains people. Around, above and beneath them." In Tel-Hai he related his work to the topography of the area, but also to its placement in the larger tectonic situation. He used heavy buldozers to create a tunnel-shaped valley, to reveal a segment of the Syrian-African Rift. He defines this geological rift as a "tectonic sculpture".

A relation to the place and to its political events was established by Tully Bauman, a member of a kibbutz in the Galilee. Using "silkprints in nature," he dealt with the recent history of the area, which means, war. On the basalt rocks that cover un underground bomb shelter, he printed cuttings from newspapers reporting shelling and violent clashes in the same area. Another artist who related to a bunker is Serge Spitzer, who in past shows dealt with observation points and pla-

SHLOMO KOREN, GROWING TREES, 1980.
UPPER GALILEE.

ces to hide. "Here," he said, "the project is a direct result of the geo-political location and historical significance of Tel-Hai. To use the settlement's shelter is therefore a natural consequence." Micha Ullman built a version of his defensive trenches, *A Settlement of Trenches,* but here directed toward the country itself, as a political act. Dov Or-Ner began in the early Seventies to do conceptual and social projects and peace performances. Later, he created the *Museum of Museums,* and started to collect information about museums. ("It's time to make the museum into a museum.") Or-Ner's project at Tel-Hai involved the conservation of information about the area. In a deep hole he buried a tape recorder with cassettes after recording people in the kibbutzim and villages. With these he conserved a bottle filled with blood taken from Arabs and Jews, and mixed together. The hole was well cemented, to be opened by the future political historians of this agitated region.

Zvi Goldstein, who returned to Israel after ten years in Milan, now uses posters as a tool for his socio-political verbal works. His belief in the future of peripheral culture is explained by the failure of the superstructures. His large posters about "Irrationa-

TEL HAI GENERAL VIEW, SEPTEMBER 1980.
IN THE FOREGROUND: **MICHA ULLMAN, SETTLEMENT OF TRENCHES.**

lism—A Crisis New Ideology" were hung at Tel-Hai in a bomb-shelter.

Avraham Ofek shifted from painting around the mid-seventies to find in Jewish culture a source for sculptural creation. Materialized verbal images and symbols taken from biblical sources and from sacred literature, produced during two thousand years of exile, became under his hands objects of mythical or ritual content. At Tel-Hai he

BATIA AROWETTI, LOCAL HISTORY, TEL HAI, 1980.
NEON AND SATIN TENT.

used the reflection of sunlight to produce light-signs on the town's walls.

Daniel Peralta is reputed for his geometrical-minimal works which are done exclusively in red and cobalt-blue. He deals with the theoretical question of visual perception. Recently, he investigated the possibilities of creating drawing lines by shadows. At Tel-Hai he executed an outdoor geometrical construction which functioned as a "receiver of light and shadow lines," as a trap in which the sunlight draws lines of shadows. David Fine, a member of a Galilean Kibbutz (born 1928) in integration with the boulders in the field, gave them the appearance of perforated, naturally eroded stones. The inclusion of the sculptor Buky Schwartz, who in the last decade has been known for his video-instrumental, new-technological works, at Tel-Hai '80 was opportune, as his project there signalled his shift toward work-in-nature and natural materials. In 1959 he initiated his connection with New English Sculpture (as a student at the St. Martin School in London), which began during that same year to consolidate around the influen-

SERGE SPITZER, INSTALLATION, TEL HAI, 1980.
METAL OBJECT, WOOD, PROJECTION, INSIDE ACTUAL BOMB SHELTER.

tial geometrical-welded sculptures of the American David Smith. Till the beginning of the Seventies Schwartz's art was based on fundamental forms, executed in metal, effectively coloured or polished, frequently based on the image of non-gravitational perception. Although always concerned with urban and architectural, or monumental, structures (such as his *Pillar of Heroism in Yad Vashem*, Jerusalem), he did some conceptual works in the early Seventies (dealing with the question of the materiality of the drawing line). This led him to the *Mirror Projects,* centered around the meaning of displacement and

IRRATIONALISM — A CRISIS NEW IDEOLOGY

ZVI GOLDSTEIN JANUARY 1980

● As long as the economic curve in western societies pointed to a constant growth in production, export and demand, and as long as the western rate of economic expansion went step-by-step with the utilization potential of the third world, these societies succeeded in building an optimistic ruling ideology, based on faith in progress and in the value of science and technology. However, the energy crisis, the crises of monetary markets, and the rocketing inflation destroyed these myths and brought about the formation of an IRRATIONAL ideology, and of an individualistic and conservative art, reinforced by the growth of a worldwide come-back to religion, withdrawal from political activity, and by the IRRATIONAL economic behavior of society.

● Inasmuch as the pre-crisis period saw RATIONALISM as the ruling ideology which succeeded in incorporating a protest antithesis, the economic crisis of today acts as a ruling factor, without leaving an alternative ideology to IRRATIONALISM. The struggle of various art media against RATIONALISM, in the name of IRRATIONALISM, is not only erroneous, but also reactionary. In spite of the claims that IRRATIONALISM is an alternative ideology, it represents today an ideological positive value against the crisis, just as the RATIONALISM represented a similar value as against the technological society. Nevertheless, it is understandable that in the technological society "par excellence", such as the American, in which RATIONALISM is more inherent than in other societies, the possibility of a confrontation between these two tendencies was not exhausted in the sixties and seventies. The conflict between RATIONALISM and IRRATIONALISM bears the danger of a new internationalization – the danger this conflict would be imposed on marginal cultural regions where the RATIONALISTIC ideology does not rule and wherein this ideology for its own sake is positive, inasmuch as it solves basic problems.

● The phenomenon of the internationalization of RATIONALISM in art in the sixties and seventies went a long way towards the cultural American imperialism. the moral lesson to be learnt from this phenomenon may prevent a second occurrence of new cultural dictates on the art of marginal regions.

ZVI GOLDSTEIN, IRRATIONALISM—A CRISIS NEW IDEOLOGY, 1980.

BUKY SCHWARTZ, YELLOW TRIANGLE, 1979.
VIDEOCONSTRUCTION.

DANIEL PERALTA, COSTRUCTION FOR LIGHT
AND SHADOW, TEL HAI, 1980. WOOD, WATER.

optical illusion. His own displacement to New York was followed by an intense activity of creating sculptures which demonstrate the failure of the eyes (parallel to mental failure) to identify, judge, and decide. His reputation in the field of closed-circuit video, is attested by John Hanhardt, who wrote in relation to Schwartz's latest work, *Yellow Triangle* at the Whitney Museum, New York: "In a reading of Buky Schwartz's Video Construction series, we can begin to explore the issues which have made his work one of the key developments in contemporary video art. Schwartz has returned his art to the immediate experience of the viewer who discovers and explores through a deconstructive process the realities of illusion." At Tel-Hai '80, Schwartz drew a huge triangle over the hills, that can be seen as a complete triangle only from one fixed standpoint. Moving away from this viewpoint will cause the form to disintegrate. Buky's intention of covering the triangular area with a temporary white paint afforded the great scandal of the art meeting, as elements of the public, institutions, and ministers used it to attack contemporary art and its circles.

Chapter V

The
Eighties

Art in Israel stands on the frontier of contemporary Western culture. One's existence as an Israeli unites physical and political factors: the friction between the feeling of deep belonging to the place, and that of a desperate involvement with contemporary art in the West, creates the energy, language, and vitality of Israeli art today. In the recent creation of paintings, sculpture, and environmental art we can identify local parameters that include deep existential stress, protest and longing, political mockery, and the expression of cultural conflicts.

Since the beginning of the Eighties Israeli art has been shifting from epistemological and postminimal concerns to a content-oriented existentialism; from esoteric conceptual disciplines toward extra-artistic situational content, and more directly, from the history of art to the history of a specific place at a given time.

The attempt to theorize the phenomenon of new painting in Israel entails dealing with circumstances and developments that characterize the country's socio-cultural and political reality. As art does not develop a history that is detached from the political context in which it is created, we find a correlation between the present crisis of leadership, economy, and politics, and the crisis of the avant-garde, which has given birth to the new spirit of art in the Eighties. This correlation is strongly emphasized in contemporary art in Israel, where the political crisis has shaken confidence in the rationality and continuity of progress in art. Narcissism has been replaced by a concern for immediate reality; and even in their most personal, introspective work Israeli artists are voicing a shared experience. Because of these characteristics the relevant work done in Israel today may be considered idealistic art, according to the definition set forth in the preceding chapters. The "genetic" impossibility of detaching itself from current existential circumstances, in other words the determination to delve deeper into the specific problems of the Israeli situation consciously, culturally, and politically, is shared by the young generation of "new painters" and the generation that made its reputation during the Sixties and Seventies. Thus the changing face of art in Israel in the Eighties has not been caused exclusively by the emerging generation of artists—those who are having their first shows in the "new spirit of our time"—but it is also the result of a radical change in the creation of mature artists dealing with painting, sculpture, postminimalism, and environmental art.

The new phase of painting in Israel at the beginning of the Eighties has occurred at the same time as that of the Western centres of art; but in Israel it also marks a turning point in local history: for the first time in thirty years painting has detached itself from the Oedipus complex of the dominant New Horizons group, which originated in the late Forties and steered Israeli art toward abstraction and the International Style. The new expressionistic tendency has given birth to a kaleidoscopic image of tension and catastrophe, affliction and self-pity, sacrifice and antiheroism. A re-examination of conscience and political myths, and a reevaluation of the meaning of existence in this land have been stimulated by traumatic events: the 1973 Kippur War; the 1977 elections, which transferred the majority from the traditional socialist regime to a right-wing nationalistic power for the first time in the brief history of this state; and the Lebanese War, which flared up in 1982.

The Israeli artist, ever conscious of being a part of a whole, and being involved in a down-to-earth way in his immediate environment, has been drawn to a turbulence of radical subjectivity, which in this context means an emotional reaction resulting from an analytical interpretation of the oppressive change in political and social reality. So that relevant Israeli art created since the late Seventies is pronouncedly self-contained and different in its sources and associations from that created in the West, despite the obvious resemblance and correlation in time and imagery.

The motif of sacrifice has become central in the recent works of certain prominent Israeli artists, as an expression of identity involving national and personal despair—which they convey by means of mythological metaphors of the irrationality of human fate. The bloody red, highly expressive paintings of Moshe Gershuni reveal a disgorging process of biographical self-destruction and insanity parallel to the insanity and catastrophe of reality itself. Anger and self-pity, mercy and protest, are sunken in rivers of blood and spittle, in an obsessive, energetic action painting that recalls the actionism of Arnulf Rainer, the radical slaughterhouse art of Hermann Nitsch, and the tormented Crucifixions of Grunewald ("don't forget to keep

MENASHE KADISHMAN, SACRIFICE OF ISAAC, 1985. IRON. COURTESY R. & D. GOTTESMAN.

a wound open"), which brings Thomas Deecke to write: "Therefore and despite their Jewish-Israeli themes, Gershuni's works are paradigms for an existence at the edge of hell." The ambiguous and paradoxical heritage of German culture and the vanished Jewish European intellectual existence of the first half of our century, being a building block of Israeli culture (an island of Western culture in the East, a haven for the Holocaust refugees) was first formulated by Gershuni in his 1980's installations. Through the last five years it has taken on a symbolic visuality of swastikas and stars of David, contaminated in a hysteric flow of blood and fire, burning flags and remnants of army emblems, from which bold sentences and words in Hebrew emerge, strikingly charged with catastrophe and despair. The Hebrew letters, as in remnants of burned scrolls, are combined to form quotes from old prayers, national hymns with strophes like obsessive laments blessing the beloved soldier in his departure to war, and to Isaac on his way to sacrifice.

Over the last few years this unification of cultural myth and the immediate situation of sacrificing one's sons in recent wars (phrases like "Terrific soldier Isaac. Yesterday you were still here, where are you now?" appear in Gershuni's work) has also become the central theme of the paintings and figurative monumental sculptures of Menashe Kadishman; and both Kadishman and Gershuni (along with Uri Lifshitz) are precedents of the young generation of painters, so many of whom have emerged since the beginning of the Eighties.

Gershuni's paintings recall esthetically

MOSHE GERSHUNI, THE EVIL WORK, 1986. MIXED MEDIA ON PAPER.

URI LIFSHITZ, UNTITLED, 1984.
ETCHING. COURTESY GORDON GALLERY, TEL-AVIV.

distorted Jewish manuscripts from the Middle Ages (which, in the education of the Israelis, bear the association of darkness, pogroms, persecutions, and horrors). Like these manuscripts, which today are documents of an epoch, Gershuni's paintings are formulated as witnesses of the present dark days of the artist's immediate environment, using biblical sentences of the prophets ("In that day will rise up the tabernacle of David that is fallen"), combining expressions of tragedy in art history, about the artist as a sacrifice, here represented by Van Gogh ("Isaac, Isaac. My soldier. Where is Vincent?").

The paintings that Menashe Kadishman executed as an immediate reaction to the eruption of the War in Lebanon, between 1982 and 1985, firmly established the theme of sacrifice in recent Israeli art. In this multi-variable cycle of large-scale canvases, the *Sacrifice Paintings*, shown extensively in Israel and abroad, Kadishman expresses his hunger for a burst of colour, executed by energetic brush strokes loaded with fauve-bright paints, in a dynamism like cleaving the rock to find the golden vein. The urgency of his concerns about current existential events in his homeland are as intensive as the poetic energy that radiates from his canvases. Pierre Restany has written: "painting produces a magical effect in Kadishman's eye: it poeticizes a moment in nature."

The drama that occurs in the *Sacrifice Paintings* goes hand-in-hand with the essence of reality. The artist is pressured between the canvas and the flow of events, as their reflection accumulates on the painting support urgently and forcefully through a surprising metamorphosis. The paintings are loaded with a wide range of cultural and existential associations, political involvement and per-

MENASHE KADISHMAN, PROMETHEUS, 1987. CORTEN STEEL.

sonal experience. They represent the search for a language that will formulate these experiences, a search to decipher the code of fate. The biblical formulation of the Sacrifice of Isaac in Kadishman's paintings is in its essence a radiation of protest, in the same land where the myth of Abraham leading his son to Mount Moriah was created thousands of years ago, and which, as a humanistic symbol, challenged thinkers and artists such as Kierkegaard, Caravaggio, and Rembrandt. This myth is repeated as a terrifying echo in contemporary reality, where the departure of the sons to war is repeated as a present ritual.

The ever-sacrificed Isaac, in every chapter of human history, is the victim of ancient rituals, as he is the victim of the contemporary ritual of war. The myth of the sacrifice, not as a philosophical or literary heritage, but as a biographical fact, explains Kadishman's attachment to this theme during the last five years.

This cycle of paintings led, at the beginning of 1985, to the realization of large-scale sculptures done in sharp-cut, rough iron plates, following the cut-out shapes of the trees in his *Negative Forests* executed during the Seventies. In these recent sculptures, the ram celebrates his victory over the sacrificed Isaac. No angel saves the son. Reality triumphs over the biblical miracle.

In the midst of ambivalence between love

IVAN SCHWEBEL, THE ISRAELIS CELEBRATE THE VICTORY OF DAVID'S FORCES AGAINST THOSE OF HIS REBELLIOUS SON ABSALOM. THEY HAVE YET TO SEE HIS SORROW OVER THE DEATH OF HIS SON, A SORROW GREATER THAN HIS FEELING FOR VICTORY (2 SAMUEL; 19,1), 1983. OIL ON CANVAS.

and sorrow, a deep nostalgic sense leads him toward a point where no bridging can occur between the yearning for beauty and perfection, and the power of destiny. Kadishman creates his works as an attempt to bring redemption. As he writes: "The sheep, the Zion Square series grew out of the Lebanese a beloved site, a place of intimacy in the land of Israel. All these have become a symbol, because the reality that gave birth to the memories has disappeared. The romantic reality becomes a longing and a symbol. We need both longing and symbols in times of loneliness, when the roots have gone from us and vanished."

Kadishman's passage to painting in the late Seventies was shared both by Gershuni and by younger artists like Gabi Klazmer and Michal Na'aman, who previously had produced important works during the conceptual era in Israel. But for two "easel painters" of his generation (born in the Thirties), Uri Lifshitz and Ivan Schwebel, the recent decade caused only a change or variability of subject matter.

Uri Lifschitz, in his virtuosic expressionistic paintings, has always radiated aggression and violence, accompanied by a touch of humour as a defense against pomposity (as seen in his sequences of boxers and heavy motorcycle riders). His reaction toward the depressed atmosphere during the continuing unwanted war in Lebanon gave birth to a series of large-scale etchings on the theme of slaughterhouses, along with images of torture and aggression based on everyday banalities such as a visit to the dentist or a mother and her (beaten) child.

The contemporary Israeli artist's intention to search for a language that will express this immediate friction between existential stress in his specific environment, and his art concepts and affinities, is apparent throughout the Eighties (as it was apparent along its relevant creation from the beginning of the century). The scholar's intention to relate Israeli art only to the model of historical German Expressionism and to its recent revivals (in the case of Kadishman and of the young Jacob Mishori), to the Graffiti art of Keith Haring (in the works of David Reeb), to Caravaggio and Goya (in the easel paintings of Ivan Schwebel) or to the Russian

DAVID REEB, YELLOW GREEN LINE WITH SOLDIER AND CHILD, 1986. ACRYLIC ON CANVAS.

JACOB MISHORI, UNTITLED, 1983. OIL ON CANVAS. COURTESY JULIE M. GALLERY, TEL-AVIV.

Avant-garde (in relation to Zvi Goldstein's constructions), is one-sided, and misses the uniqueness that characterizes recent Israeli creation.

Ivan Schwebel grew up in New York, but has lived in Jerusalem since 1963. In his published diary he relates the process of creating his series of paintings in which biblical scenes of King David's saga are presented today in the Square of Jerusalem. In this diary we find direct references to the ambiguity of painterly values contaminated with existential urges: "The notes in my journals concerning the Zion Square series, grew out of the Lebanese War in June, 1982. The action takes place in the center of modern Jerusalem, that is, West Jerusalem, an area built and used by modern Israel in recent times. Without any literary or religious sophistication I simply implant a scene from the Book of Samuel onto the street (the Israelis celebrate the victory of David's forces against those of his rebellious son Abshalom. They have yet to see his sorrow over the death of his son, a sorrow greater than his feeling of victory). I may have missed placing events by a half kilometre or so. The quality of the summer sun in Jerusalem cuts like I remembered it during my first years here. White to yellow to red on blue. Paint with it, and the war goes away. The reds

begin to dance instead of bleed. . . . Here's David showing a toothy smile with penetrating eyes (in the scene of David and Uriah), white emphasized, besides the body theatrics I use. I don't want to push the impersonal quality too far away. Besides, I recall precise facial expressions in Piero della Francesca's figures which even serve the impersonal. . . . This Caravaggesque behaviour lights me up. Paint mixes with psychological forces as never before.

"In the face of the real disasters befalling Israel, do I seek to make paint despair? There are few moments when the red evokes blood, but far more that touch the potential apocalyptic nature of events."

This "apocalyptic nature of events" radiates also from the combine works of Bianka Eshel-Geshuni, which the artist began to produce in 1980, and which reached their peak five years later. Her work exemplifies the process of creating a visual syntax as an outlet of psychological stress and a desperate lamentation on existence, love, and belief. The only salvation, in this context, can be reached by the transformation of any small remnant, any found object or personal souvenir, to a form of radical beauty, like a talisman against death and approaching disasters. Plastic flowers, fruits, and small figures, fake

115

banal jewellery, women's stockings, stuffed birds, gold-coloured leaves and feathers, personal photographs, lead soldiers, and golden candy wrappers, tar and streams of red-sticky bloody colour, are part of her nontraditional art materials. Bianka is collecting childhood fairy tales, nightmares, and vague visions of Provoslavian altars, to take part in her black carnival of the poor, in the obscure ritual of kitsch and despair. In her recent works, human-size crucified, crushed figures hang over a landscape of small graves and dead bluebirds. Bianka Eshel-Geshuni's postmodern esthetic has developed a personal language that has no precedent in local art.

The prevailing return to painting, which has changed the inner landscape of artists' studios, galleries, and museum exhibition spaces in Israel, was already established in 1981 (by the mega-show of Kadishman's new expressionistic paintings and a group show, *A Turning Point*, in the Tel-Aviv Museum; and by gallery shows of Moshe Gershuni and Jacob Mishori, among others). This phenomenon embraces a wide range of approaches to subject matter and painterly values.

Jacob Mishori, in his works from the early Eighties, used flat, fresh colours to paint aggressive portraits, which he set against a background of frightening symbols of enigmatic ruling regimes. He expressed ambiguity and perplexity in a combination of transsexual visions and scenes of cruelty, containing soldiers, wild dogs, and bombardments of stalags or military camps. With a brush charged with rage he protested against an unidentified situation of danger and oppression. His radical symbolism and expressionistic technique—which represented a departure from the tradition of painting in Israel and from that of Seventies postminimalism—was objected to by the local museums, even in the case of group shows of new painting. His paintings of 1985, showing an affinity to the "wild" German expressionists, have become darker; they represent his own figure against the background of deserted and isolated cityscapes. A similar interest in achieving radical, expressionistic images of eroticism and violence through "corrected" self-portraits, has

TSIBI GEVA, UM AL-FAHEM, 1984. PAINTS ON CANVAS. COURTESY JULIE M. GALLERY, TEL-AVIV.

been shown by Yehuda Purbuchrai, who belongs to the same generation as Mishori (both artists were born in the early Fifties).

A pronounced political concern within the vogue of "new painting" is expressed by David Reeb, who has received widespread public attention since 1980. Using linear and contour methods of painting, Reeb often divides his canvases into squares to create a comic-strip-like sequence of events, reflecting cinema and television culture and utilizing the conventions of American graffiti. The themes of these works include visions of a kibbutz before and after bombardment, and oppressive urban "bankscapes" dominated by squadrons of jet fighters. His exhibition in the Tel-Aviv Museum provoked a scandal, when the museum staff objected to the huge banners in the colours of the PLO flag that had been hung for the opening. Reeb's activities since 1983 have included the organization of shows by Palestinian painters from the West Bank and Gaza (the first such projects to be realized in Israel), and a militant exhibition of Israeli and Palestinian artists entitled *Against the Occupation of the Palestinian Land* (meaning the regions conquered by Israel in the Six-Day War of 1967).

Direct ethnic, cultural, or political reference to the Arabs was quite taboo in Israeli art from the Thirties to the Seventies, although Ytzhak Danziger contributed, in a somewhat intellectual manner, to the understanding of certain aspects of Arab mythologies in Palestine. We do find overt references to the Palestinians before this time, in the art of the Twenties, when the Arab worker appeared to young artists such as Paldi and Gutman (compare above) as a strong son of the Oriental Paradise. In the Seventies we can point out sporadic works relating to the Palestinians—among them Dani Karavan's *Environment for Peace* at the 1976 Venice Biennale (where the artist included on the walls of his constructions a written declaration about the rights of the Palestinians to live in peace in their historical homeland), Pinchas Cohen Gan's tent in the refugee camp at Jericho (erected following the Six-Day War), the political art of Dor Orner (including his mixed-Jewish-and-Arab blood project at the Tel Hai '80 meeting), Micha Ullman's 1972 project for exchanging earth between an

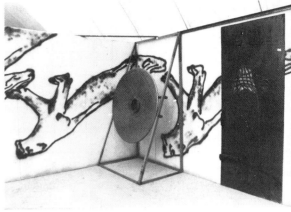

TSIBI GEVA, INSTALLATION, 1983.
METAL, SPRAY, ACRYLIC. COURTESY TEL-HAI COLLEGE.

Arab village and a kibbutz, and the works by Klazmer and Sharon, and by Gideon Gechtman, concerning "Arab work" at the 1976 *Open Workshop* sponsored by the Israel Museum. Since the early Seventies most artists have taken part in political activities calling for recognition of the Palestinians' right to self-determination and for the immediate withdrawal of Israel from the occupied territories.

Expressions related to this problematic theme exist also in the works of the young generation of the Eighties, especially in those of Tisibi Geva (born 1951). In his paintings of 1984-85, Geva synthesizes two languages: the one a muddy, ascetic, drippy colour-field painting, the other a literary, conceptual formulation of Hebrew letters indicating the names of Arab villages and Jewish sites as they are pronounced by the Arabs, and roadlike curved lines connecting these settlements—topographic metaphors for mental associations. In addition, the paintings frequently contain stereotyped figures "as would have been done by an Arab child." Geva's approach even leads him to include poignant quotes from Palestinian song in his canvases, such as "My land, my land, I shall give you all my love and all my heart." His recent paintings, done in acrylics, industrial paints, oil, lacquer, and spray paints, grow out of his indoor installations of 1981-83, in which he included the image of the *Wounded Lioness,* from a famous Assyrian statue from the Seventh Century B.C., as an expression of antiheroism. Geva recently wrote: "I search for a

DORON YAHALOM, GARDEN, 1983. IRON CONSTRUCTION AND ZINC PLATES.

definition of the environment, a private formulation which, perhaps, may incidentally become another version of the Israeli Experience. I do live here and I do believe that even a sensation of alienation, of exile, is the function of communication, of belonging."

Doron Yahalom, like Geva, is a member of a left-wing kibbutz, and like Geva he deals, in his tin reliefs and constructions, with stereotyped images of Palestinian culture, in references to the destroyed orchards of those who were compelled to flee the land (one is reminded here of the land-art work of reconstructing a devastated Arab pomegranate garden on a terrace on the side of a Galilean hill, executed in 1983 by Dov Heller). How different the effect of one theme can be on the creation of a painterly language by artists from the same generation and background, is seen in the works of Michael Kovner: the dwellings of the Palestinians in Gaza, their walls painted in bright, clean turquoise, red, blue, and yellow, have inspired in this painter a fauvist, Matisse-like Mediterranean vision. As he puts it: "I want these houses to be the first step to a painting that reflects joy and uplifting, to a painting that is inspired by the feeling of Spring."

Shuky Borkovsky has dealt obsessively,

since 1978, with the image and shape of the Kàaba stone in Mecca as a reference to Islamic culture, paradoxically a point of departure to illusive minimal design.

A sophisticated dialogue between contemporary Western culture and Islamic geometry and mathematical mysticism distinguishes Zvi Hecker, a painter and architect who developed a highly personal philosophy of polyhedral design that gave birth to some of the more widely known and controversial constructions in Israel (in 1962 the Bat-Yam

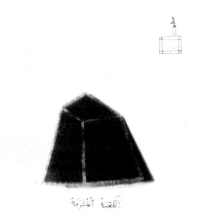

SHUKY BORKOVSKY, UNTITLED (THE KA'ABA), 1979.

118

ZVI HECKER, RAMOT HOUSING, JERUSALEM, 1980.

City Hall, with Neumann and E. Sharon; in 1969 a synagogue in the Negev; and the recent *Ramot Housing Project* near Jerusalem). The basic assumption underlying Hecker's thought and work is that the formation and structure of every organic and inorganic element of nature inevitably have a formal pattern of their own. Hence, the mere existence of a thing implies the existence of a pattern that defines its form. By choosing the polyhedron as the basic unit for a geometrical "genetic code," he creates his spatial constructions, projecting his artistic subjectivity on the objectivity of scientific observation. Hecker says: "I consider that the geometrical structures of my polyhedral works are as much reflections of scientific insight into the structure of matter as they are images invoked by the mathematical and ornamental heritage characterizing Middle Eastern culture, to which I belong." In his paintings of 1982-85, he has enlarged Islamic ornamental manuscripts with architectonic designs and calligraphic lettering, to form expressionistic, dynamic color fields.

Ryoram Merose shifted to painting at the beginning of the Eighties, after an intensive "hard core" conceptual experience in the mid-Seventies. His large-scale works and, lately, his works on paper, place the human figure in the associative space of a cynical, parodic, and hopeless opera whose libretto and stage sets seem to be coproductions of Picabia and Samuel Beckett. The sharp-cut drawing of the figure, arrested in a frame on the bright space splashed with confetti colors, is accompanied by domestic tools such as hammers, irons, and screwdrivers. The works are coupled with narrative texts, such as, "Sometimes I still see them. They come, they press, we hide in the forest," and "They make us change. They screw our arms, want us to convert. We wait." The atmosphere of absurdity and alienation becomes radical in the later works, painted mainly with tar. The script disappears and the repeated masculine figure is met by objects, most of them technical and electric in nature. The figure, half-

GABI KLAZMER, OTA, 1983. INDUSTRIAL PAINTS ON PAPER. COURTESY NEOMI GIVON, TEL-AVIV.

119

ORLY MEIBERG, FIGURE, 1985.
ACRYLIC ON CANVAS.

naked and drawn with decisive contours, is not touching any tool. Without an outlet, it takes on the role of a busy, keen proletarian who does not recognize his own existence as the script of an absurd play. This large series of paintings, which Merose calls *Happy Moments (Opera)*, bears a message of existential oppression.

The emotional staging of the large-scale paintings and installations of Miriam Neiger exploits the "flow" of industrial paints, soft materiality, and loosely designed forms loaded with sensuality and abstracted eroticism. As her 1983 installation at the Isreal Museum, *Devil's Train*, demonstrated, the visual sensation itself is the subject matter of this festive, neobaroque, organic-shaped environment. At the opposite end of the spectrum from the tactile, earthly works of Neiger are the paintings of Gabi Klazmer, who broke into the definitions of new painting to become one of its protagonists, having two shows, during 1983, in the museums of Tel-Aviv and Jerusalem. His paintings in industrial paint and acrylics bear enigmatic illusions of broad landscapes in a dusky light, against which he sets bulky objects and dark figures. This work

exists on the borderline between the visual interpretation of sublime nature, affine to Clyfford Still's abstraction, and the radiation of a dramatic and pathetic atmosphere. Klazmer describes impressive sunsets and large, strange constructions of a possible cardboard stage set. His images radiate an apocalyptic message and a feeling of alienation (due also to the large Hebrew titles written in Roman letters). Klazmer, who is still attached to the conceptual disciplines, prefers to describe his paintings of 1983 (a sequence of nonobjective "sunsets," horizontal in composition and from the point of view of the brush strokes) as "a possibility to refrain from painting and still create painting, to be mechanical in production and still touch the 'marvelous,' the 'experimental,' the 'empathetic.'" In addition to the ambiguity between the artist's intentions and the artwork's "independence" to radiate a visuality whose contents exceed the intentions of its creator, Klazmer's paintings send forth signals as from the twilight of a mythological past.

Definitely conscious of cultural mythologies as an essential component of the thematic range of her paintings is Rivka Rinn, who was educated in the Academy of Vienna and who has shown in Israel since 1983. Her forcefully drawn lines and her stormy, material color reveal a clear debt to German Expressionism. Rinn's ideas concerning the visual quotation of myths (from Eastern Mediterranean culture) touch on the need for identification with the place and examining the sentimental knot between contemporary creation and language, and the remote roots of our concepts about art making. Her intention "to start again from the beginning" leads her to deal with images created by Manet (at the dawn of modernism) and by Danziger (a turning point toward contemporay art in Israel). The bulk of her large-scale paintings done in 1984-85 represent an apocalyptic sinking of cultural remnants into flames and raging floods.

Direct involvement with mythologies is rare in the works of the young generation in Israel, as is the inclination toward radical expressionism. These artists had to break through the heritage of the relatively refined Abstract Impressionism that prevailed in the local art schools, or through the belated col-

ELI KOPLEVITCH, UNTITLED, 1984.
OIL ON CANVAS.

ELI SHAMIR, ACTEON LEAVES FOR HUNTING, 1984.
OIL ON CANVAS.

lagist abstraction of other dominant teachers. The veteran expressionists who emigrated to Israel from Central Europe in the early 1930s were fogotten long ago. In this context, saturated expressionistic paintings like those of the young Orly Maiberg (born in 1958, returned from art studies in New York in 1984) constitute a fresh phenomenon, as do the psychological figurative paintings of Eli Koplevitch and Rachel Rabinowitz, both kibbutz members. (In an important group show, recently mounted at the Museum Ein Harod, including forty-six young artists, more than half were born in, were educated at, or lived in, kibbutzim. This fact seems to be more than a statistical datum).

The heavily drawn figures in the sombre earthly paintings of Eli Shamir transmit a sensation of ritual events of a rescued community, of an obscure earth myth. The direct looks of his figures bear warnings, accusation, and danger. Differently staged, the groups of soldiers in the field which obsessively inhabit the canvases of Pamela Levy, look—from the point of view of their subject matter—like a daily report on the Israeli landscape. This fact in itself is loaded with enough anxiety to make the image of the tan, half-naked soldiers vibrate against the background of the sun-scorched soil. These vibrations, transmitted by the artist to the canvas and reflected to the perceptive eye, create subconscious impressions of hidden disaster. The minute, impressionistic brush strokes and the muted colors create a frame of restrained hysterics around the impact of the subject.

The "soldiers in the landscape" in the paintings of Moshe Mirsky, done in a quick and impatient hand, bear witness to the personal experience of this young artist who, like others in his generation in Israel, is a soldier when needed.

The fear of war was directly expressed in Joshua Neustein's open-air project for Tel-Hai 1983. Neustein, a protagonist of conceptual and postminimal art in Israel in the late Sixties, burned into the soil of the Galilee (near the border of Lebanon, beyond which the war still raged) a full-scale shadow of a jet fighter. Every day, for a fraction of a second, the real shadow of jet planes hurrying to the north loaded with missiles overlapped his imagined shadow. (A correlation exists between this project and his *Jerusalem River Project* realized in 1970: along a dry river bed leading from Jerusalem toward the Judean Desert he implanted tens of small loudspeakers that transmitted the sound of streaming waters. An external effect gave the dry river the impact of a streaming reality.) As a parallel to the "shadow" work, Neustein showed his *Map* paintings, which were followed by a sequence of huge paintings (the development of which is still in progress) showing maps of the world as seen from his studio. Neustein, the "refugee artist" after his own definition, is installed in a nonplace, as the world is seen from his window; a large fan, fixed on the ceiling above him, creates a beam of air that does not mix with the surrounding air— refugee air for a refugee artist in a nonplace. By another definition, the only homeland of the artist is his studio, his art.

The image of war refugees dominates a series of expressionistic paintings made by Alma Ben Porat after a long period of executing works that sardonically parodize nationalistic stereotypes and visual slogans of heroism for the masses. Also, many artists in the Eighties have, like Neustein, included direct references to jet fighters in their works. The young Dudu Mezak has made installations, utilizing metals and artificial lighting, in which war planes are suspended over mini-constructions of camps (similar images appeared in the paintings of Jacob Mishori). Dov Orner, in his obsessive political art, has created dozens of projects, from 1970 to the present, in which an antiwar message is trenchantly expressed. In reaction to the War in Lebanon he used olive branches to build a full-scale model of a jet fighter attached to a model of the bomb that destroyed Nagasaki —a symbol of disaster and fear without precedent in the history of humankind. The impact of this work by Orner, installed in the Galilee hills overlooking the frontier with Lebanon in 1983, was anticipated by a cycle of works correlating hands which appear in the painting of El Greco with the artificial arms of a war invalid, as though analyzing art history from the standpoint of the battlefield. All of his recent projects are excerpts from his *War Museum.* ("The cardinal problem of our age is the perpetual development of the Art of War. It becomes more and more   sophisti-

MOSHE MIRSKY, SOLDIERS, 1985.
OIL ON CANVAS.

JOSHUA NEUSTEIN, STILL LIFE, 1983.
AIRPLANE SHAPE, BURNT RUBBER ON EARTH, ON THE LEBANON BORDER.

DOV OR NER, JET FIGHTER, 1983.
DONE OF OLIVE TREE BRANCHES, SCALE 1:1.

cated and destructive.")

This nightmarish sense of reality is shared by Chaim Maor, who in the same year made an installation in black wood repoducing the Auschwitz concentration camp. Maor, the son of a prisoner in this death camp, is not the only member of the young generation of the Eighties to touch openly on the question of the Holocaust. These works, with their "poor" materiality and urgent execution, constitute what may be called "aesthetic rejectionism."

David Frumer "attacks" the reality of a sophisticated war through the visual language of computerized video games. Frumer's canvases bear the colorful sweet vibrations of the popular electronic games, whose landscapes are inhabited by tanks, jets, and soldiers. Frumer cynically relates to this reality of horrors-as-games, accompanied by the rhythms of imaginary space explosions and the multiple decibals of heavy rock, by combining in his paintings the aesthetics of graffiti, Fauvism, and Dubuffet's "brut" design.

The shift to painting by the young conceptualists of the Seventies was never detached from a rational questioning of the meaning of painting itself. This approach is well exemplified by the paintings done by Michal Na'-aman since the late Seventies. Her colors and forms, more than expressing retinal sensation and painterly values, serve as tools in her consistent investigation of the enigmatic and axiomatic sources of cause and effect, and of words, forms, and meanings. Genealogical and Darwinistic representations of the human figure (based visually on Goya's paintings, *The Little Giants* and *The Greasy Pole*), rhyming between remote forms (such as the turtle and the human brain), eggs and chickens, and ape-men, are accompanied by phrases such as "The face he had before the world was made" and "The eye that sees itself." Her paintings deal with the representation of nonvisual terms such as "spiritual beauty" or the "subconscious," which are indispensable to visual language. This pseudo-scientific visual research is shared by Pinchas Cohen Gan in the scientific-like aesthetic of representation with which he parodies Euclidian geometry in his installations of "non-Euclidean" bodies, as well as in his paintings. Cohen Gan reaches high painterly values by dealing with questions of human scale versus space, colour fields and volumes as components of art syntax. In the recent works of these artists, epistemological analysis and doubts about the potentiality of artistic language are absorbed as though by osmosis from their works of the seventies, and combined with reflections of immediate reality (as in Michal Na'aman's painting, *New Young Victim*).

The radicalization of fragmentary vision and discontinuous imagery is the basic concept of Yudith Levin's painting on found, used plywood and masonite supports. She combines a "poor," casual aesthetic with the

HAIM MAOR, A MESSAGE FROM AUSCHWIZ TO TEL HAI, 1983. WOOD INSTALLATION.

MICHAL NA'AMAN, BLOOD CONNECTION, 1982.
PAINTS ON PLYWOOD.

YUDITH LEVIN, AMOR AND PSYCHE, 1983.
ACRYLIC ON PLYWOOD. COURTESY KNOEDLER, ZÜRICH.

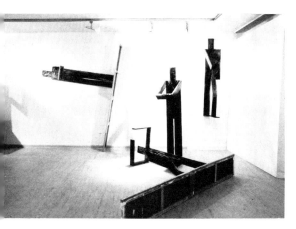

YORAM AFEK, FIGURES, 1983.
INSTALLATION IN WOOD, CLAY, PAINTS.

JACK JANO, PORTRAITS, 1984.
PAINTED WOOD.

richness of colourful brush strokes inherited from the expressionistic tradition. A loosely figurative design on scattered plywood fragments attached to the wall force the eye to assemble the image across the voids. Some of the works bear quotations from art history, and others contain images of danger and doubt. A fragmentary vision of the world is one of the essentials of modern art. It contradicts the wholeness and harmony of the Renaissance vision, which expresses the belief in a unifying power of justice and security.

The divided brush strokes of the impressionists, the cubist collages, the combines of Robert Rauschenberg, and the broken-plate supports of Julian Schnabel—all herald or witness the collapse of the belief in heavenly or earthly authority. This concept is expressed well in the works of Yudith Levin, in the layered collage paintings of Tamar Geter, in the painted wood reliefs and installations of Nair Kremer (whose "visual opera" sees joy and disaster in an ambiguous light), and in the coloured, fragmentary wood sculp-

TERESA GEJER, IN MEMORY OF, 1984-85. PLYWOOD, CLAY, PLASTER.

126

tures of Jack Gano, who creates totemlike figures in rituals of fear.

The idea of sculpture in nature, using materials from nature itself to capture the meaning of the "place," its mythological, historical, and existential concepts, dominates sculpture in Israel in the mid-Eighties. It is accompanied by a significant shift of postminimal sculptors toward extra-artistic content, namely toward a concern for the inherent stress of their environment. Micha Ullman digs his shelter trenches in hard rocks, and places on it a tilted chair in stone or mud, which symbolizes a collapsing "throne." Mud and compressed earth are, after Ullman's definition, "the stuff from which the huts in the refugee camps are made." The representation of the image of sky, in his recent drawings, refers to a feeling of prayer in an absence of outlet. In a 1985 project, he reinforced a volume of earth with iron. The sense of hiding and sheltering is expressed in such an exhaustion as to charge a metaphysical feeling into a bulk of earth.

Hava Mehutan, in her works executed in 1984 in the Dead Sea desert and in Jerusalem, is more directly concerned with war and death. In these works Mehutan, who has lived in a desert town since the late Forties, created

ADINA BAR-ON, IN PERFORMANCE, 1983.

wood and stone sculptures embodying torsos. Only recently she has begun to combine these torsos in environmental works surrounded by sandbags. Rows of trenches with sandbags executed in the desert convey a sense of tragedy and disaster. ("The rows of holes in the ground and the sandbags are arranged so as to suggest that there is no end to the holes to be dug.") Young artists such as Noam Rabinowitz are joining, in the eighties, this trend of using materials from nature to make works in the open with a message about the place and its sentimental or historical meaning.

The use of figurative languages that communicate existential stress was largely detailed in connection with the sacrifice sculpture of Kadishman. The young Yoram Afek shifted around 1982 to wood constructions covered with thick, colorful paint, which relate to figure positions in installations that radiate a content of war and sheltering. The rectangular design of these figures suggests robots who act under order of dehumanization. The muddy camouflaging and tactile values of the wood planes refine the alienation of the scene.

In a strategy of staging a colourful human circus Moti Mizrahi testifies to the insanity of a society: on the roof of the Tel-Aviv Museum, floating sweet-coloured sculptures of happy acrobats and armed soldiers create a visual opera of ambiguities and understatements.

A like shift from ascetic performances to a rich vision in the Eighties, characterizes the recent works of Adina Bar On. At the Tel Hai Meeting of 1983 she presented, in the open, in an installation of water, light, and sounds, a new approach to dramatic performance based on existential and psychological subject matter. The work was entitled *A Woman in War.*

The turning phase of postminimalist and epistemological sculptors toward extra-artistic contents was clarified in 1982, in a show of six sculptors held in Tel-Aviv.

Nahum Tevet, in his floor-wall constructions and installations, done over the last four years, uses the modernistic language that characterizes his wooden multiple structures of transparent space inside a given space. But now, free from the dictums of the Seventies, his works include chairs, rounded painted

PENNY YASSOUR, RECURRENCE, 1984. COLTH, WAX, STRAW AND EARTH.

MICHA ULLMAN, SKY, 1983. LIMESTONE.

DAVID FINE, ARC, 1983. BASALT.

HAVA MEHUTAN, FIELD, 1984. WOOD AND SAND SACKS.

YAACOV DORCHIN, AN ANGEL IN AN IRISH
LANDSCAPE (DETAIL), 1983. COMBINED SCULPTURE.

plywood plates, disks, and mainly covering the materiality with paints. His constructions free themselves from the floor and "climb" on the walls. They exist in a floating position, creating associations of space vehicles and sensations of cosmic space, with its disintegrated coloured components. This approach reacts against the computerized high-technological masks of contemporary human beings, who will always remain poets, dreamers, and children (he uses kindergarten coloured chairs). These works need to be read gradually. Their complicated wooden arms, sticks, and convex lines that hold different-sized ready-made wood nets and chairs, look like a machine that will never work. A Picabian humor is transformed here, together with quotations from Monet's lily-ponds in Giverny (by the painting of the rounded wood plates) and iconlike gold and blue shapes. These imaginative cosmic vehicles float over and reflect the world below. They may bring to our mind an illusionary escape from a reality that lost its promised land.

In his constructions of the Seventies, the spectator was encircled by the multiplied structures. Now, in the recent, baroquish works, the eye perceives them from the outside. But in both cases, we witness Tevet's obsession with conveying a schizophrenic existence through an abstracted understated language.

Michael Gitlin's turn toward a version of postminimalist expressionism, still retains the materiality of the massive wood, but substitutes the decisiveness of the hand-made impression (characteristic of his displacement-relocation works throughout the

DRORA DOMINEY, UNTITLED 1984.
WOOD CONSTRUCTION..

YEHUDA PORBUCHRAI, UNTITLED, 1986.
ACRYLIC, OIL AND PASTEL ON CANVAS.

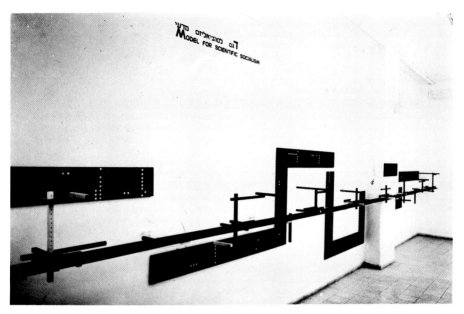

ZVI GOLDSTEIN, THE ESTHETICS AS MODEL FOR A SCIENTIFIC SOCIALISM, 1982.
COURTESY GIMEL GALLERY, JERUSALEM.

Seventies), with a covering of painted plaster that encases the wood, creating mummified figures and dangerous passages between sharpened forms.

Drora Dominey, who first exhibited in 1982, presents a different approach by creating coloured wood (mainly wall) sculptures, which are based on the forms of industrial utilitarian carpentry. She avoids any organic visual elements, for the sake of integrating the values of art and function.

The intention to use pronounced materiality and industrial relics and objects for the creation of bold expressionistic effects, is seen in the recent works of Yàacov Dorchin. It seems that Dorchin's main interest is the power that is reflected by materiality, and the aggressive (or delicate) effect created by combining raw industrial "signs of energy." In a large work executed in 1983, he combines coarse, used, massive elements of iron and wood with a found human skull. In order to avoid any interpretation of the events in his environment, he entitled this assemblage *An Angel in an Irish Landscape*. The work can represent an altar on which all the energy, human and industrial, is gathered together for the creation of an art sensation full of power and urgency.

Zvi Goldstein, in the mid Eighties, diverted part of his verbal energy to metal sculptural objects that are situated on the border line between functional industrial products and abstract metal artworks. His concern with aligning a concise three-dimensional form with a linguistic one, to complete a political-artistic message, is one of the most intriguing developments on the local scene in recent years. Goldstein is referring to

MICHAEL GITLIN, ENCLOSURE, 1982.
MIXED MEDIA ON WOOD.

131

BUKY SCHWARZ, THREE ANGELS OF COORDINATION FOR MONITORING THE LABYRINTHIAN SPACE, 1986.

the Russian Avant-garde (in the overall aesthetic of his work and by clear reference to Tatlin in his *Model for Socialism* executed in 1984) to symbolize a possibility of creating a new artistic language. The polished treatment of the objects compares with the careful choice of a sentence in one of his geocultural manifestos. Throughout his work Goldstein attempts to prepare a conceptual art-revolution, for which he uses the strategy of the art trend that accompienied the October Revolution.

Buky Schwartz, whose contribution to video art we detailed in previous chapters, turned in the early Eighties from his video didactic illusionism to works in nature, using natural materials, such as tree trunks, and dispensing with intermediaries between the viewer and the form produced. In other recent works, he creates—by the means of mirror displacements—a single, unitary painting from its different parts scattered on the walls of a space. His guiding principle is invariably that the definite existence of a fact is dependent upon our attitude toward it. His use of eucalyptus trunks, leaning against the wall and connected to it by bright patches of paint arid by drawn lines, has an existential content of leaning, attaching, and connecting.

Only in 1982, Dani Karavan had his first one-man show in an Israeli museum (at the Tel-Aviv Museum; until now he has not shown at the Israel Museum in Jerusalem, nor has any work of his been included in its collection). Also, he is creating his first outdoor sculpture-as-monument in Tel-Aviv, his native city. Karavan has done his largest projects for urban spaces over the last few years—namely, his three-kilometer axial project for the new city of Cergy-Pontoise near Paris (along which twelve sculptural stations will create an art environment of unprecedented dimensions); and his recent project for the central square of the New Ludwig Museum in Cologne. In both cases Karavan has followed some basic principles of environmental art: to integrate the work with the given land—or cityscape; not to impose forms, but to reveal the main relations of the site with its environment; and to point out or emphasize these existing relations using the most delicate materials and means to realize his intentions (laser beams as drawings in space, a line of streaming water, the sound of the wind, the shadows cast by sunlight). In his exhibitions during the Eighties he took from

DAVID SCHVILI, ABOUT A JUNGLE, 1984. OIL ON CANVAS.

YASCHA CYRINSKY, UNTITLED, 1986. WOOD, PLYWOOD.

NAHUM TEVET, BOAT, BRIDGE AND
YELLOW CHAIR, 1984.

nature soft materials such as sand, water, and
light as drawing through fine apertures
between raw wood plates. Karavan's style
reflects his moral concepts about art, society,
and nature.

A radical approach to art as a modernistic
product of a progressive avant-garde philosophy that goes hand-in-hand with the most
advanced achievements of technology, and

therefore negates any mystical, nostalgic, and
postmodern tendencies, is represented by the
surprising plans of Ezra Orion to create
"sculpture in the solar system."

In May 1984, at a symposium held in
Jerusalem in connection with an exhibition
entitled *Eighty Years of Sculpture in Israel* at
the Israel Museum, Ezra Orion launched his
ambitious project to install a sculpture on the
planet Mars, utilizing the equipment of the
spacecraft Viking I, which landed the red
planet in 1976, and that of the Mars Rover,
which will land on it at the end of this decade.
This declaration, which appears to duplicate
the energy of the Futurist Manifesto ("everything moves, everything rotates, everything
occurs at a dizzy speed"), is a "quantum leap"
with respect to Orion's obsessive creation of
the past fiftieen years (suffice it to recall his
tectonic desert sculptures, executed in the
Israeli desert, and the 1981-83 project in
which he created a large-scale "runway" of
slate in the Himalayan Annapurna basin, at
an altititude of 4000 meters).

Orion, now in the process of organizing
the logistics of his project in the solar system
(which involve institutions like NASA) writes:
"Matter comprises undulating fields of
energy. It is now a departure from the visual-
material realization of sculpture, and its per-

NOAM RABINOWITZ, EROSION, 1985. BASALT.

EZRA ORION, TOWARDS THE ANNAPURNA, 1981-83.

ception as acts of energy via the obtuse abstract achievements of tele-field power, tele-ranges and the velocities of light."

As we have seen in these pages, the main bulk of the art created in Israel from 1906 on has been political and ideological in content, although it has shared many stylistic features with the Western art scene. In the compli- cated geo-political problems which Israel has to face and the deep concerns of the artists in Israel toward their environment, there is no doubt that basically political interest will con- tinue to crop up in art, for in Israel perhaps more than anywhere else on the globe, artistic expression is an integral part of the all- encompassing concept of existential creation.

ZEEV RABAN, RUTH, 1920's.
PAINTING ON GLASS. COLLECTION M. KADISHMAN.

REUVEN RUBIN, THE FAMILY, 1927.
COLLECTION TEL-AVIV MUSEUM.

ISRAEL PALDI, PORT OF JAFFA, 1920's.
COLLECTION R. PALDEI.

JOSSEF ZARITSKY, TREES IN JERUSALEM, 1926.
WATERCOLOR. COURTESY GORDON GALLERY, TEL-AVIV.

NAHUM GUTMAN, THE GOATHERED, 1926.
OIL ON CANVAS.

MOSHE CASTEL, SHABBATH REST, 1938.
COURTESY GORDON GALLERY, TEL-AVIV.

MENAHEM SHEMI (SCHMIDT), FISHERMEN, 1928.
COLLECTION TEL-AVIV MUSEUM.

YITZAHK FRENKEL, SYNAGOGUE IN SAFED, 1939.
COLLECTION ISRAEL MUSEUM, JERUSALEM.

MOSHE MOKADY,
TWO FIGURES, 1940's.

ELSA LASKER-SCHULER, FIGURES IN JERUSALEM, 1940.
COLLECTION ISRAEL MUSEUM, JERUSALEM.

MORDECHAI ARDON,
NEAR JERUSALEM, 1944.

YOSL BERGNER, BUTTERFLY EATERS, 1965.
COLLECTION W. SHAMSKY, ST. LOUIS.

YEHEZKEL STREICHMAN. FIGURE AND INTERIOR. 1950.
OIL ON CANVAS.

AVIGDOR STEMATSKY, SUMMER, 1966.
OIL ON CANVAS.

ITZHAK DANZINGER, NIMROD, 1939.
NUBIAN SANDSTONE.
COURTESY ISRAEL MUSEUM, JERUSALEM.

ZVI MAIROVICH,
WINDOW WITH ORANGE BLOSSOM, 1972.

YOHANAN SIMON,
SABBATH AT THE KIBBUTZ, 1949.

MARCEL JANCO, WOUNDED SOLDIER IN THE NIGHT,
1949. OIL ON CARDBOARD.

ARIE AROCH, BUS IN THE MOUNTAINS, 1955.
OIL ON CANVAS.

AVIGDOR ARIKHA, NOIRE BASSE, 1959.
OIL ON CANVAS. COLLECTION ISRAEL MUSEUM, JERUSALEM.

ORI RAIZMAN,
ROAD IN THE DESERT, 1970.

LEA NIKEL, PAINTING, 1973.
COLLECTION TEL-AVIV MUSEUM.

ELIAHU GAT, LANDSCAPE, 1972.
OIL ON CANVAS.

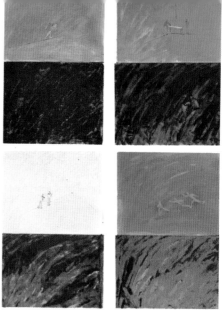

IVAN SCHWEBEL,
THE ARTIST AND HIS FRIENDS, 1971.

PINCHAS COHEN GAN, ABSTRACT PAINTING,
FIGURATIVE SPACE, TIME PERCEPTION (DETAIL), 1973-77.

URI LIFSHITZ, ANONYMITY, 1967.
OIL ON CANVAS. COURTESY GORDON GALLERY, TEL-AVIV.

MOSHE KUPFERMAN, UNTITLED, 1964.
OIL ON CANVAS. COLLECTION J. HACKMEY, TEL-AVIV.

AHMA, ABSTRACT, 1970's.
ACRYLIC ON CANVAS.

RAFFI LAVIE, PAINTING, 1971.
COLLECTION GILAT, JERUSALEM.

LILIANE KLAPISCH, THE WINDOWS, 1970.
OIL ON CANVAS, COLLECTION ISRAEL MUSEUM, JERUSALEM.

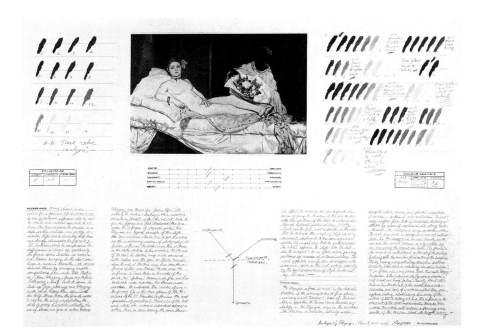

OSVALDO ROMBERG.
MYTHOLOGIES: FROM ALTAMIRA TO MANET, 1980.

MOSHE GERSHUNI, VINCENT EFFECT, 1981.
MIXED MEDIA ON PAPER.

DANI KARAVAN,
LEIZER LINE, TEL HAI, 1980.

EZRA ORION, TOWARDS THE RIFT, TEL HAI, 1980.
250 METERS EARTH WORK.

BIANCA ESHEL GERSHUNI, THIS HOME IS FULL OF LOVE, 1981.
FEATHERS, ARTIFICIAL BIRD, OIL-PAINT PASTE, DRY COLORED ROSES, PLASTIC PUPPETS.

MENASHE KADISHMAN, THE LAST SUPPER, 1981.
OIL ON CANVAS.

MICHAEL KOVNER, GROUP OF HOUSES WITH A CAR IN GAZA, 1981.
OIL ON CANVAS. COURTESY BINET, TEL-AVIV.

**IVAN SCHWEBEL, THE BIGGEST EVENT OF
THE YOUNG NATION - DAVID, HAVING CONQUERED
JERUSALEM BRINGS IN THE ARC OF THE COVENANT
JAFFA ROAD, ACCOMPANIED BY TWO LIONS
AND A PEUGEOT, 1983.** OIL ON CANVAS.

TSIBI GEVA, BILADY BILADY, 1985.
PAINTS ON CANVAS. COURTESY JULIE M. GALLERY, ...

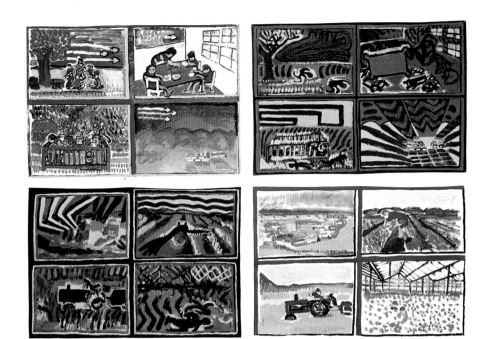

DAVID REEB, UNTITLED (BEFORE & AFTER), 1983.
COURTESY DVIR GALLERY, TEL-AVIV.

ZVI HECKER, SPIRALE, 1983/84.
PAINTS ON CANVAS.

JACOB MISHORI, UNTITLED, 1983.
OIL ON CANVAS. COURTESY JULIE M. GALLERY, TEL-AVIV.

RYORAM MEROSE, HAPPY MOMENTS, 1984.
PAINTS AND ASPHALT ON WOOD.

JOSHUA NEUSTEIN, FAN OVER THE MIDDLE EAST, 1982.
ACRYLIC ON PAPER.

LARRY ABRAMSON, LANDSCAPE PAINTING, 1983.
ACRYLIC ON WOOD.

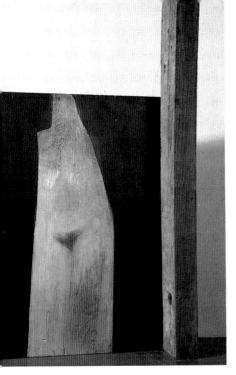

MICHAEL GROSS,
FEMALE NUDE AND WOODEN LOG II, 1982.

NAHUM TEVET, WAS IT PURPLE ON RED?, 1986.
PAINTED WOOD CONSTRUCTION.

DAVID SHVILI, WESTERN PIECES AND CHINESE OUTLOOK, 1986.
OIL ON LINEN.

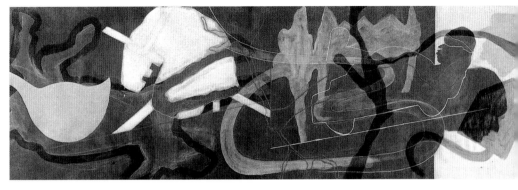

TAMAR GETTER, SLOPES, 1981.
ACRYLIC, LACQUER AND OIL CHALCKS ON CANVAS.

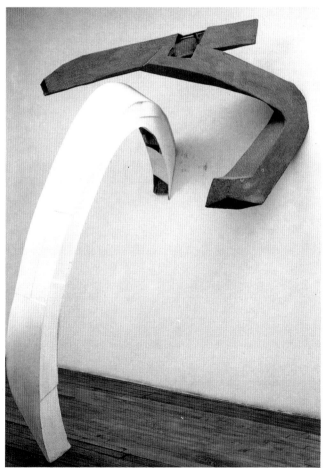

MICHAEL GITLIN, ENCROACHED ARC, 1984.
ACRYLIC AND PLASTER ON PLYWOOD AND WOOD.

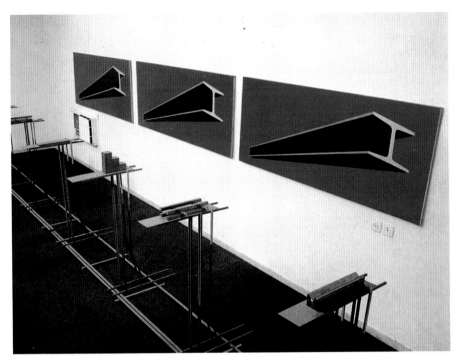

ZVI GOLDSTEIN, FUNCTION, PROGRESS AND UNIVERSALISM IN THE THIRD WORLD, 1982.
METAL, WOOD AND PAINTED PANELS.

PINCHAS COHEN GAN, THE OTHER SCIENCE IN GREY, 1982.
ACRYLIC ON CARDBOARD AND WOOD.

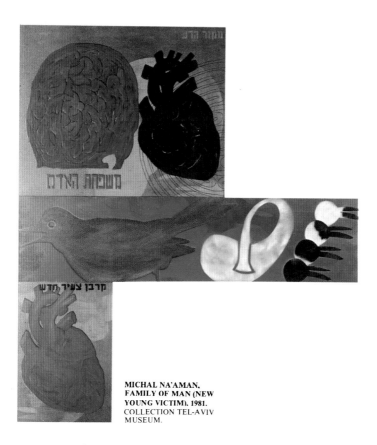

**MICHAL NA'AMAN,
FAMILY OF MAN (NEW
YOUNG VICTIM), 1981.**
COLLECTION TEL-AVIV
MUSEUM.

YUDITH LEVIN, THE LAST GRACE, 1982.
ACRYLIC AND CHALK ON PLYWOOD. COURTESY KNOEDLER, ZÜRICH.

MIRIAM NEIGER, UNTITLED, 1983.
ACRYLIC AND SPRAY ON PAPER. COURTESY GIMEL GALLERY, JERUSALEM.

SHAOUL SMIRA, NEMESIS, 1986.
MIXED MEDIA.

ALMA BEN PORAT, FROM THE SERIES "RITUALS AND REFUGEES",1984.
OIL ON CANVAS.

HAVA MEHUTAN, HARSDOM, 1984.
TRENCHES AND SAND SACKS.

DINA RECANATI, PARCHMENTS, 1984.
PAINTED WOOD VENEERS.

YITZACK LIVNEH, DAY AND NIGHT, 1986.
ACRYLIC ON CANVAS.

DAVID FRUMER, WAR GAMES, 1983.
OIL PASTELS.

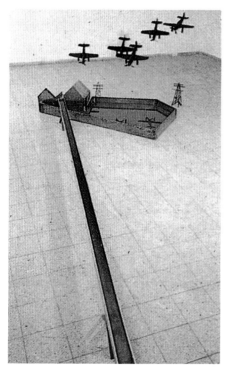

DUDU MEZAK, ENVIRONMENT, 1984.
WOOD, PLEXIGLASS, PAINT, WATER.

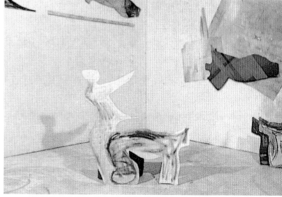

**NAIR KREMER, INSTALLATION AT THE SAO PAULO
BIENNIAL (DETAIL), 1985.** PAINTED PLYWOOD.

•YEHUDA PORBUCHRAI, UNTITLED, 1986.
ACRYLIC, PASTEL AND OIL ON CANVAS. COURTESY JULIE M. GALLERY, TEL-AVIV.

RIVKA RINN, DEJEUNER SUR L'HERBE, 1984.
OIL ON CANVAS. COLLECTION K. NAGLER, VIENNA.

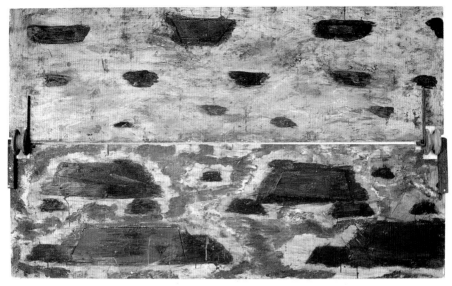

YASCHA CYRINSKY, 1986.
MIXED TECHNIQUE ON WOOD RELIEF.

PAMELA LEVY, SOLDIER, YELLOW, 1983.
ACRYLIC ON CANVAS.

DORIT FELDMAN, COMBINED WORK
1984. INSTALLATION.

SHAUL SHATZ, MERAV, 1980.
OIL ON CANVAS. COLLECTION TEL-AVIV MUSEUM.

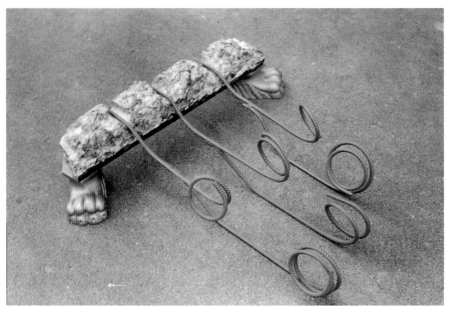

ISRAEL RABINOVITZ, UNTITLED, 1987.
IRON, WOOD, GRANITE.

Special Thanks to:

The Israel Museum, Jerusalem; Tel-Aviv Museum; Gordon Gallery
and Shia Yariv; Julie M. Gallery, Tel-Aviv; Tel Hai Contemporary Art Meetings;
G. Talpir Archive and to Joseph Hackmey.

Photo Credits:

Yàakov Agor, Ran Erde, Avraham Hay, D. James Dee, Israel Zafrir,
Yoram Lehman, David Rubinger, Peter Rosenberg, Nahum Slapek,
Reuven Milon, David Harris, Peter Szmug, Beny Karmazin,
Alex Agor, Ephraim Erde, Moshe Shai, Haim Lusky, Menucha Brafman.

Summary